Entrepreneurial Foundations For Twenty and Thirty Somethings

Steven A. Hitz

Foreword by James L. Parke
President & CEO
OtterBox

Although the author and publisher have made every effort to ensure the information and ideas contained in this book were complete upon publication, they do not assume, and thereby disclaim, any liability to any party for any loss, damage, or disruption caused by errors or omissions, wherever such errors or omissions may exist. Further, this book is meant to serve as a collection of strategies and ideas that have proven effective in the personal experiences of all contributing authors. However, the author, publisher, and Launching Leaders Worldwide, Inc. make no representations or warranties with respect to the accuracy or completeness of the contents of this book, and specifically disclaim any implied warranties of personal, professional, or financial success. Summaries, strategies, and tips are only recommendations by the authors, and reading this book does not guarantee one's results will exactly mirror the results achieved by contributing authors.

Book cover and interior design by Fly, New Zealand
Editing by Charles Limley
First Edition

Printed in the United States of America

ISBN-10: 1-7322906-0-1
ISBN-13: 978-1-7322906-0-0

If you are an aspiring entrepreneur, you will benefit greatly from reading and applying the principles outlined in this book. Steve Hitz teaches practical lessons based on entrepreneurial experience and real life expertise. The concrete applications will greatly benefit the enterprising "go-getter."

—Brent M.T. Keele, President, Blue Ocean Enterprises Inc.

Having just finished my undergraduate degree, Entrepreneurial Foundations effectively articulates the internal struggle I have been facing. Do I join the rank and file at a reputable company or do I set off determined to blaze a trail of my own? Steve effectively communicates the benefits and opportunities inherent to the entrepreneurial path, without glossing over the risks and challenges. Entrepreneurial Foundations not only informs those thinking about starting their own business, but also acts as a guidebook for those who are ready to take the plunge.

—Alex Leonard, Business Consultant

Entrepreneurial Foundations presents a young-hearted and vibrant approach to entrepreneurship, giving readers a unique combination of modern thinking and business insight, combined with proven and hard-learned lessons from the author's personal experience as an entrepreneur. Steve Hitz has spelled out the foundational truths of success, both for your business and for yourself as a businessperson. This book gives you powerful guidelines as you embark on this exciting journey, progressing from the initial "entrepreneurial itch" through the struggles and glories along the way.

—Hinna Maluch, Projects Coordinator

Reading this book couldn't have been more timely, considering my personal situation as a refugee. I recommend Entrepreneurial Foundations to anyone who wants to experience a better life, not merely through making money in business, but through changing your perceptions, identifying your strengths, and redefining your core values.

—Amir Raki, Refugee Response Coordinator

The writing style is so refreshing—like having a conversation with a trusted friend. No extra content to meet publisher's requirements, just insights based on experience that seem so obviously relevant and helpful to anyone who might want to be an entrepreneur. I'll definitely be coming back to this again.

—Stephen Schraedel, Business Operations Analyst

Another great book from Steve Hitz! I appreciate his ability to paint the picture of his experience as an entrepreneur clearly and powerfully, discussing some of the challenges he has faced and giving readers insights into how he achieved success. He makes the entrepreneurial experience real by including his personal experiences alongside powerful business lessons and suggestions for further reading.

—Jesse Olsen, Software Engineer

Dedication

As I stepped away from the "electronic pen" of my computer's word processor, having finished my work and turned it over to my professional editor, Charles Limley, an overwhelming sense of gratitude for all my entrepreneurial mentors washed over me. Then, I sat down and enjoyed a bowl of Cap'n Crunch cereal (you'll understand the importance of this when you finish the book).

I hope the principles outlined in these pages will serve as a tribute to my mentors and a guide to my readers. May the influence of this book be sweeter and longer-lasting than even the best bowl of Cap'n Crunch.

Author's Note

Entrepreneurial Foundations was conceived as a curricular cornerstone of Launching Leaders Worldwide, a nonprofit organization that teaches personal development and leadership principles to the rising generations. Founded in 2008 by a group of successful entrepreneurs, business executives, and teachers—all of whom are also people of faith—Launching Leaders Worldwide is particularly focused on empowering participants to connect their personal and professional growth with faith, weaving all aspects of life into a holistic daily walk.

You will see references to Launching Leaders throughout this book, and you are invited to participate in any of its courses to learn about and engage more deeply with its curriculum, regardless of your religious background, status, or affiliation.

Ultimately, this book presents a wide range of topics that my colleagues and I believe are relevant to young entrepreneurs. If you are looking for spreadsheets, data dumps, or mechanisms for number crunching, this is not the book for you. But if you are interested in foundational principles that will guide and enable you to build a successful entrepreneurial life, then this is exactly what you're looking for.

The ideas you are about to encounter are designed to give you a framework that can be adapted to your unique circumstances and goals, and that will consistently point you toward a better life.

Welcome. It's time to take the leap!

Table of Contents

Foreword

For an airplane to reach its destination, someone has to fly the plane. Many people idly daydream about flying, but few have paid the price of effort and boldness to become a pilot. In spite of that fact, we all benefit when well-trained pilots do their jobs. Most of us take for granted the remarkable things we are able to accomplish when expert pilots allow us to reach new heights with a level of safety that we could never achieve on our own.

Similarly, in the business world, many people dream of running their own business and being their own boss. Few people have the courage to actually do it. Those who do are brave individuals with the good fortune and foresight to see opportunity where others see only obstacles. They have the confidence to try something new and the resolve to start again after missteps. The ripple effects of this boldness create prosperity and economic stability for the rest of us. The label society gives to these ambitious souls is the French word: "entrepreneur."

This book, *Entrepreneurial Foundations for 20- and 30-Somethings*, is a powerful tool for anybody who has desires to become an entrepreneur—especially those of the rising generations.

Entrepreneurs innately focus on creation, innovation, and new ideas. It is their willingness to dream that allows them to succeed, for as the old adage goes, "if you can't dream it, you can't achieve it." Principled entrepreneurship—which is what this book is all about—combines the ability to create with clear values and healthy motives. Principled entrepreneurship changes lives, communities, and in a few instances, has even influenced the course of history. Most people will never realize the debt they owe to entrepreneurs. The truth is that the seeds of the success and stability we enjoy as a society were, and continue to be, planted by entrepreneurs.

In my career as an attorney and executive I have had the opportunity to interact with many talented entrepreneurs. I have noticed patterns in their successes and commonalities in their failures (and most entrepreneurs experience varying degrees of failure before they find success). I have observed that what distinguishes entrepreneurs from everyone else is not their intelligence, not their education, and certainly not their discipline—it is their attitude toward risk and their ability to dream.

The most successful entrepreneurs I know resorted to entrepreneurship because they weren't fulfilled being an employee or a traditional student. Entrepreneurs are often visionaries that quickly move from one idea to another. They are comfortable with ambiguity and typically too impatient to enjoy repetitive tasks. Before an entrepreneur makes it big, society myopically looks down on them because they don't seem to fit into our typical educational or employment environments—and thank goodness they don't. It is an entrepreneur's restlessness and unwillingness to conform that leads them to pursue ideas and opportunity, and that leads them to create wealth and abundance where others see only risk and fear.

Like a pilot, entrepreneurs allow the rest of us to achieve levels of prosperity and peace of mind that would otherwise be unattainable. Turning a great idea into a functioning company is like building a plane while attempting to fly it at the same time. Throughout the process, the plane of entrepreneurship will need major overhauls, maintenance, and renovations in mid-air to effectively serve its customers. This is a task that seems dangerous or even reckless to most people but fills a true entrepreneur with excitement.

The path of entrepreneurship is full of self-doubt, heartache, failure, second attempts, and incremental successes. Many would-be entrepreneurs bow out before realizing their dreams because they have not developed the stability of character and values required to support their enormously challenging journeys. That is where Launching Leaders steps in—giving budding entrepreneurs the tools they need to become who they want to be, so that they can focus their efforts on building what they were destined to create.

The principles outlined in this book are not new or unique; they are time-tested and proven ingredients in the recipe for lasting, balanced success. Steve Hitz is a wonderful example of the success and happiness that comes from principled entrepreneurship. Through Launching Leaders, he has found a way to share important themes that make a difference in the lives of people all over the world. I have met with participants in Launching Leaders courses and have seen lives changed by these principles. More directly, I can say with confidence that the topics presented in this book, such as responsibly managing money, selecting the right team, focusing on people and culture, and having a purpose beyond profit, have made all the difference in my own career.

It should be noted, as it is later in this book, that entrepreneurship is not for everyone. Every successful entrepreneur needs a talented team of accountants, lawyers, human resource professionals, marketers, salespeople, engineers, software developers, etc. to support his or her efforts to achieve success. There is just as much dignity (and significantly more security) in a more traditional profession as there is in entrepreneurship.

Many failed businesses are started by people who want to be entrepreneurs, but don't have the stamina to withstand the turbulence and adversity that inevitably come in pursuing a great idea. If, however, you find that entrepreneurship is your path, then this book is your flight plan as you begin your journey to success.

James L. Parke
President & CEO
OtterBox

Introduction

"The journey is never ending. There's always [going to] be growth, improvement, adversity; you just [have to] take it all in and do what's right, continue to grow, continue to live in the moment."

—Antonio Brown[1]

One of the primary reasons I am writing this book is because I think of myself as a Baby Boomer with a Millennial heart. Even though I'm older than you, there is so much about your generation that I find praiseworthy and inspiring, and now that I'm approaching the retirement phase of my life, I believe I have some powerful insights and knowledge to share.

This book is intended for 20- and 30-somethings who want to become entrepreneurs. My expertise on the subject comes from firsthand, real-world experiences—both the successes and the failures. My wife, Ginger, and I have been entrepreneurs for almost our entire adult lives. We raised all five of our Millennial-age children in a home where dinner time looked more like a board meeting than a normal family meal. I guess the process of launching several businesses over the course of 30 years will do that to a family. Today, our kids are grown up and they are all either active entrepreneurs or working toward becoming entrepreneurs.

I'm grateful that things worked out for our family, but looking back, I realize that we spent so much of our home life talking about business and work that we probably let things get a little out of balance during our kids' growing-up years. This was one of the many mistakes I made as we tried to figure out the entrepreneurial life. We didn't have a manual or a road map to follow as we blazed new trails and established new highways. We took things one day at a time, tried to learn as much as we could, and figured things out as we went.

Now, after learning how to navigate all this, I have a lot to say. I've had the great opportunity to learn from incredible mentors and to pull wisdom from life-changing books and authors. And, of course, I learned my most priceless lessons from the school of hard knocks. In each of my business ventures, I put it all on the line. I felt every profit and every loss deep in my gut. After decades of risk, hard work, and riding the ups and downs of the entrepreneurial life, I've pieced together a uniquely powerful set of tools, principles, insights, and information that will empower anyone to succeed.

I hope my purpose for writing this book is not because I'm subconsciously searching for relevance during my retirement years. I hope my purpose is to give you and other entrepreneurial-minded 20- and 30-somethings the tools you need to succeed, to achieve your financial goals, and most importantly, to accomplish it all while living authentic, holistic, and meaningful lives that align with your individual faith, belief, or value system—whatever it may be. Simply put, this book will give you an exceptional foundation as you venture out into the world of risk and reward known as entrepreneurship.

Millennials Were Born to Be Entrepreneurs

In 2013, a writer named Joel Stein wrote an article about Millennials that was published in Time magazine. In it, he argued that Millennials are "narcissistic, overconfident, entitled, and lazy," "fame-obsessed," "convinced of their own greatness," and "stunted."[2]

You've probably heard these kinds of negative stereotypes about Millennials before. Unfortunately, ideas like this have become fairly common—but they couldn't be more wrong. Over the past 30 years, I've employed over 10,000 Millennials, mentored many from your generation, and have even helped several 20- and 30-somethings launch their own businesses. Through all these interactions, I've had the great opportunity to get to know numerous young adults on a profoundly personal level. I've discovered that I resonate deeply with the way your generation thinks about the world and about life—especially when it comes to work, jobs, money, and giving back. I actually prefer your generation's mindset on these matters over my own.

In this book, I use the terms "20- and 30-somethings," "Millennials," and "the rising generations" interchangeably, as a way to describe very generally your generation. I do not intend for these to be reductive or pejorative labels, and I hope that my use of these terms is not taken as an attempt to squeeze you or your generation into a pre-defined box. I have great respect for folks in your generation, and hope to contribute something of value to you.

In fact, the more I've thought about it, the more I've come to believe that far from being self-obsessed, lazy failures, Millennials are actually poised to become the greatest generation of entrepreneurs the world has ever seen. You are living in some of the toughest economic times since the Great Depression and the job market you are entering is vastly different from—and much more difficult than—the one your parents were born into. I won't sugar coat the challenges you face or try to paint a rainbow unicorn picture of the world for you. But I will say that in an unexpected way, all these challenges have actually given your generation a unique set of tools that will prepare you for entrepreneurial success—if you learn how to harness them.

For example, the economic uncertainties you've faced for most of your life have conditioned and prepared you to cope with the financial risk and instability that always comes with life as an entrepreneur. Similarly, I've noticed that people in your generation tend to prioritize integrity and staying true to their personal values. Millennials generally focus on relationships, interpersonal connections, and the pursuit of meaningful life experiences more than making money.

As a result, Millennials know much more than just how to survive rough financial swings. Millennials know how to stay aligned with their most important personal values. They intuitively understand that people are more important than profits. Millennials know how to learn on the fly, adapt as they go, and maintain a sense of adventure.

These are the basic building blocks for becoming a truly successful entrepreneur. This book will teach you how to put these blocks together so you can build something beautiful. My goal in writing this book is to marry the powerful independence and smarts so many Millennials naturally possess with proven keys and wisdom that will empower you and your generation to become the most successful—and the most joyful—entrepreneurs of all time.

The Entrepreneurial Life

The word "livelihood" is intriguing to me. The Merriam-Webster dictionary defines it simply as a person's "means of support or subsistence."[3] As I've thought about it, however, I think the word also hints at something much larger than mere subsistence. To me, true livelihood isn't about just getting by. It's about how you live your life and the quality of the life you live. It's about cultivating a meaningful, authentic, values-based life rather than mindlessly floating on auto-pilot.

For many people, the entrepreneurial life offers the best route to true livelihood. This isn't to say that pursuing a professional life not geared toward building your own business is inferior. Please understand that while I believe everyone has the potential to become a successful entrepreneur, I also understand that there is a large percentage of the population who will never explore that opportunity.

I have immense respect for those whose desire is to be the best employee they can possibly be, and who love the security of a regular job. The world needs all types of workers and building a career as an employee is honorable and much-needed. The world wouldn't function without a diverse mix of people, some of whom want to be entrepreneurs and others who want to be employees.

If you would rather focus on building a career as an employee, then God bless you—you are making a powerful difference in the world. With that said, this book is written for Millennials who have the entrepreneurial itch but who don't know how to scratch it. If you're in this category, I understand how you feel. For many of us, putting in regular hours working in somebody else's business feels too much like just getting by. Those of us with this mindset often feel like a wild animal stuck in a cage—we understand that you can't keep a tiger in a cubicle. This book is designed to give you the knowledge you need to break free.

The entrepreneurial life offers some truly incredible benefits and opportunities. In my experience, the most empowering aspects of becoming an entrepreneur include:

- The ability to take more control of your life.

- A unique sense of job security as you learn to trust yourself, your ideas, and your capabilities.

- Incredible personal growth.

- The chance to break down externally-imposed constraints to pursue non-traditional paths.

- The opportunity to dismantle corporate hierarchies.

- Freedom to re-negotiate your reality.

- The chance to create your own flair.

- The resources to make a difference in the world and give back on your terms.

Key Concepts for Success

Before we get started, there are a couple key concepts you need to keep in mind. The first is understanding that an essential piece of achieving true livelihood—rather than merely scraping by—is to make a living doing something that you love.

If we figure that the average full-time worker puts in 40 hours per week, and we assume that most workers get five weeks of paid leave per year, we can estimate that we spend an average of 1,880 hours working every year. That equates to more than 92,000 hours, or roughly 35% of a 50-year-long adult life. How miserable would you be devoting that much of your life to something you despise? Unfortunately, too many people resign themselves to this fate. I know many people who hate their jobs and who constantly complain about them. Fortunately, I believe that being an entrepreneur is the best way to avoid this.

The other foundational concept you need to understand is that all success—whether general life success or success as an entrepreneur—hinges on staying true to your core values. My previous book, *Launching Leaders: An Empowering Journey for a New Generation*, provides a detailed, step-by-step guide for identifying and building a personalized set of core values and a clear plan for your life.[4] I highly recommend reading that book first, as it will give you a strong foundation for implementing the concepts explained in this book.

One way or another, you need to take time to figure out what specific values and ideals matter most to you. What kind of person do you want to be? What specific qualities, attributes, beliefs, and practices will help you become that person? The answers to these questions will help you figure out your core values.

Similarly, if you are a religious person, or if you follow any sort of spiritual tradition, then your faith can help you identify your core values. I strongly encourage you to cultivate a solid connection between your faith and your everyday walk, including your professional work. The belief that true success as an entrepreneur comes when you live the same standards and values across all aspects of your life is at the foundation of everything I share in this book. Whatever your faith is, weave it into everything you do as an entrepreneur and you will find yourself on the path to true livelihood.

Let's Get Going!

Trail Ridge Road winds its way through the heart of Rocky Mountain National Park, not far from where I live in Colorado. Reaching elevations as high as 12,183 feet, this road is closed during the winter because the snow often builds up to 20 feet deep or more. The road is so high up that the air is always cold, even in the summer.

One of my favorite things to do is drive to the very top of Trail Ridge Road, park in the pull-out, and hike up the short public trail. Once I'm at the pinnacle of the trail, I face the wind, close my eyes, stretch out my arms, and breath in the purest air on earth.

This is rarified air. It refreshes my soul and gives me a sense of freedom and inner peace. It awakens my spirit and body, and somehow, I feel cleansed. After a few minutes of this beautiful solitude, I walk back to my car, my cheeks red from the crisp air, my heart pounding from walking at high altitude, and an invigorating smile on my face.

In a very real way, this is how it feels to enter the entrepreneurial path. Honestly, even this metaphor doesn't do justice to the excitement of becoming an entrepreneur. The only way to really understand what I'm talking about is to dive in and experience it for yourself.

Let's get going!

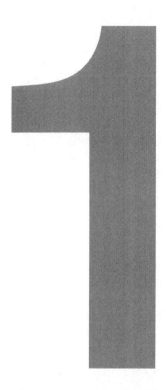

Why on Earth Would You Want to Become an Entrepreneur?

"I have never thought of writing for reputation and honor. What I have in my heart must come out; that is the reason I compose."

—Ludwig van Beethoven[5]

When I was 29, I had a solid and secure job working for a relatively large national company. I was rapidly climbing the corporate ladder and had recently been promoted from field rep to regional manager. On top of that, I had been named either employee of the year or manager of the year for several years in a row. At the height of my achievements with this company, I was making a six-figure income, driving a new car, had just purchased our first home, and was putting money into our savings account. Simply put, I was living the dream.

Yet I still felt deeply unfulfilled. I was constantly frustrated and I felt stuck. I couldn't implement my own ideas without first running them through the company's convoluted, slow-moving bureaucracy, and a lot of the time, my ideas were shot down anyway. If I pushed too hard against the status quo, my superiors became angry. Sometimes they threatened to fire me.

I soon found myself weighed down by the sense that I was wasting away in this corporate stranglehold. I felt my independence being stifled. Although this job was safe, secure, and enabled me to provide for my family, I could no longer watch my ideas and energy wilt on the vine before producing any fruit. More and more, I felt that I simply could not plant or nourish anything meaningful as long as I was trapped in someone else's greenhouse. It became painfully clear that the corporate setting I found myself in was dominated by people more interested in protecting their turf and building silos than in constructing something meaningful that could make a positive impact on the world.

There is nothing unique about this situation. In fact, there are a surprisingly large number of people who feel just as unsatisfied with their jobs as I did. As recently as 2014, the Conference Board, a New York-based nonprofit research firm, found that the majority of all Americans are unhappy in their current jobs.[6] Given the fact that we all spend a large portion of our adult lives working, this level of unhappiness and dissatisfaction is definitely disturbing.

But is being frustrated with your job enough to quit and set out on your own? That was one of the many questions I asked myself at the height of my unhappiness. I also wondered if I was being prideful. Was my ego getting in the way of good sense? Was I being selfish and focusing too much on my own desires? Why on earth would I jeopardize such a solid, secure job and risk everything to start my own business?

I eventually realized that I needed to weigh my personal frustrations against my ability to make a living and put food on the table for my family. Simply being frustrated or unhappy was not enough to take the leap, and many people in my life thought it would be a very bad idea to trade a steady job for the uncertainties of starting my own company. After all, the path of an entrepreneur is full of risk, and most startups are doomed for failure. In fact, 80-90% of all startups fail within their first five years, and 80-90% of those that survive the first five years end up folding shortly thereafter.

I knew these statistics when I was contemplating the idea of leaving my current job to start my own business, and I was careful to include these risk factors in my considerations. I also carefully considered my ability to move into a specific business niche that I could monetize effectively. I thought about how much I already knew and tried to identify the specific knowledge and skills I would still need to acquire in order to succeed. I chewed on all this for quite some time—it was at least a couple of years before I took any concrete action.

Ultimately, I needed some prodding to help make up my mind. At the height of my turmoil over what I should do, I was asked to travel to my employer's headquarters for an important meeting. Given the success I'd been having in my job, I (perhaps arrogantly) assumed I was being called in for another massive promotion. I asked my wife, Ginger, to travel with me and as we sat on the airplane from Los Angeles to Kansas City, we daydreamed about the juicy corporate job I was so sure I was about to be offered. We even started looking at real estate and talking about neighborhoods and schools for our kids.

I was shocked when I discovered that the "important meeting" was nothing more than the company owner's wife lecturing me about how I'd overstepped my role by paying $20 a month for a new water cooler without first getting approval. She made it clear that I was not to spend one penny without first receiving authorization. It hit me that the expense of flying me all the way to Kansas City was more than enough to pay for two years of the water cooler I'd just gotten in trouble for installing. Clearly, this was not about helping the business. It was about power, control, and internal politics, and I wanted nothing to do with any of it.

On the flight back home, I decided it was time to break the corporate handcuffs and set out on my own. I'd done my research, weighed the risk factors, and reached the conclusion that I had what it takes to succeed. Obviously, there would be numerous risks completely beyond my control, but I felt that I'd prepared myself as much as possible.

Above all, I knew that my current work environment was not sustainable. Not only was it professionally and personally unfulfilling, it was becoming a significant presence in my life—in a negative way. Making matters worse,

I was being pulled into petty political fights that were now impinging on my ability to focus on my job. It was time for me to set out on my own, build my own company, implement my own ideas, build my own team, and create the kind of work environment where I and the rest of my team could truly succeed. I wanted to make an impact on the world in my own personal and unique way.

Shortly after the meeting in Kansas City, I left my job and started my own business. Even now, as I look back on this journey and as I remember what it was like to start my own company for the very first time, my stomach does backflips. I never took lightly the decision to become an entrepreneur, and I will forever be grateful that I eventually decided to take the plunge.

As you consider this possibility in your own life, think about your current situation and compare it to what you most deeply want to do and accomplish. Consider your unique set of skills, knowledge, and expertise and weigh it all against the risks you will face. After thinking through it all, if you still have a burning, unstoppable passion for blazing your own path through life, then it's time to get started.

While it is absolutely essential to prepare as much as you can, understand that sooner or later you simply have to go for it. You will always feel underprepared and inadequate; it comes with the territory. But putting forth sincere effort to learn and prepare yourself first—which includes reading this book—will give you a solid foundation on which you can build a successful entrepreneurial career.

One day, a student from a Launching Leaders class I was teaching asked to meet with me for breakfast. This student—we'll call him CJ—was a very bright college graduate. At the time, he had a steady job working at a car dealership. It seemed like a great position, but as we ate together, CJ told me that he felt deeply unfulfilled. In fact, he felt it was time for him to move on to something new. He was already in the process of trying to figure out his next step in life.

Chapter Summary

- The decision to become an entrepreneur is a big deal. Don't take it lightly, but don't overthink it—at some point you have to take the plunge!

- Meditate on the reasons why you would consider becoming an entrepreneur. Are you ready to take on the world of risk and reward in which every entrepreneur lives?

- Make sure you're not making a rash decision based on petty personal grievances.

- To be fully committed to your vision and your business, you must be driven by the right motives.

Find What Fits:
How to Tell If
Entrepreneurship
Is Right for You

"When I let go of who I am, I became what I might be."
—*Lao Tzu*[7]

CJ had been floating his resume around for a few months and had just been given a final interview with a global defense contractor. The job sounded like a perfect fit, as it would allow him to use the sales and marketing skills he learned in college and would open doors for significant advancement in his field.

I was about to advise him to go for the interview when he added: "But I also have an opportunity to go to Laguna Beach, California." I asked him what he would do there. "I don't know exactly," he answered. "But I have a friend who I can stay with while I figure it out." The more we talked, the more it became clear that CJ's heart was leading him toward the Laguna Beach option.

It was then and there that I gained an important insight into the mindset of many in the rising generations. CJ was intent on following his heart—regardless of where it led him or what practical sense it made. He was willing to give up a job that would pay him twice his current salary, with benefits and all the trimmings a career-path job, in exchange for a vague and undefined hope. He knew from his past experiences what he did not want in terms of a career path, and he was willing to forego the "security" of the defense contractor job in order to explore the unknown.

Many people from older generations might call CJ irresponsible for even considering the Laguna Beach idea. Some might see it as evidence that Millennials are out of touch with reality or that they lack the work ethic required to maintain a full-time job. But that's not how I see it. CJ wasn't being immature or selfish. He was refusing to be defined by anybody else's expectations or by externally-imposed notions of responsibility or respectability. He was so determined to forge his own way through life that he was willing to bypass a secure job that he knew would make him miserable.

I actually applaud his willingness to go with his gut. To be sure, the details of the Laguna Beach idea needed to be filled in at some point, but many times in life, it's best to work in broad brush strokes, trusting that the details will work themselves out as you go. This kind of decision-making is powerful because it requires you to use both your head and your heart. It forces you to prioritize the hope of a bright future over the mundane path of subsistence, even if it means diving into something without first knowing each and every detail. This is exactly what CJ was doing.

In many ways, I think CJ represents a lot of Millennials. Your generation often cares more about cultivating meaningful life experiences and finding ways to make a difference than trying to grind out a living. Generally speaking, Millennials demand control over the decision-making process, whether it's at work or in their personal lives. You want to have an active say in what happens in your life and you are not content to follow the aspirations, expectations, or visions that other people have for you.

These attitudes align very closely with the type of entrepreneurship you will learn about in this book. More than any generation before you, Millennials want to contribute something to the world, not just take from it. Likewise, the framework for entrepreneurial success outlined in these pages is centered on having a purpose and striving to make a positive difference in the world. Implementing the principles taught in this book will empower you to live the life you most desire, including the ability to determine your own schedule, bring to life your own ideas in your own unique way, change course at a moment's notice, rise above the restrictions of corporate bureaucracy, and engage like-minded associates in a cause bigger than yourself.

Find What Fits

While the path of an entrepreneur will open up incredible opportunities, it's not the only path through life. As I mentioned in the Introduction, there is no shame in choosing to work for somebody else. In fact, this can be an equally honorable way to build a meaningful career that also makes a positive impact.

At the same time, I also believe that anybody can learn how to become a successful entrepreneur. Even if you're not the most naturally talented businessperson, learning correct principles and then putting in the hard work to implement those principles can enable you to succeed.

The key is figuring out which option is the best fit for you as a unique individual. The root of entrepreneurism should never be reactionary. In other words, it's never a good idea to set out on this path if your only reasons for doing so are personal grievances, frustrations, or anger. Yes, these emotions can confirm your decision, but they shouldn't be the sole reason you become an entrepreneur.

Instead, your entrepreneurial path should arise out of heartfelt and sincere desires that resonate deep inside you. This is another reason why I admire the ability of Millennials like CJ to put so much trust in their gut. It's also a key reason I believe so strongly in the power of weaving faith and spirituality into your professional life.

Many spiritual traditions place a strong emphasis on "following your gut," which is sometimes called "following the Spirit," "listening to your heart," or pursuing your "calling" in life. Whether or not you adhere to a religion or spiritual tradition, the point I'm trying to make is that you need to dig deep and ask yourself why you want to become an entrepreneur. If you're fully honest with yourself, you'll know the answer—you'll feel it in your soul.

To help you navigate this process, here are some of the biggest reasons people choose to become entrepreneurs, as well as some of the reasons people choose to pursue other professional paths. Take time to review each of them, and then think about what you really want. And remember, one path is not necessarily better than the other. It's all about discovering what's right for you, being willing to follow your gut, and committing yourself to whichever path you choose.

Reasons to Become an Entrepreneur

- **Unique opportunities for personal growth** – When I was a small plane pilot, I had to be prepared for any possible scenario, from unpredictable turbulence to engine failure. The level of understanding required to be this prepared could not be downloaded from the Internet. The only way to acquire it was to actually do it. I put in thousands of hours of study, practice, and most importantly, time in the air.

  Being an entrepreneur is very similar. When you are the owner and leader of a business, the buck stops with you, which means you must be prepared to handle just about anything. And while studying is an absolute prerequisite for success, a lot of what you learn will be out in the real world, while you're living the experience. This process is definitely challenging, but there is nothing more rewarding. Your personal growth will be exponential—especially if you remain humble and teachable.

- **Control your time and destiny** – Every entrepreneur will tell you that hard work and long hours are part of the gig, especially in the early years of a new business. However, as an entrepreneur, you get to decide where, when, and how you spend your time. As a business owner, you decide where your time will best be spent, and you get to determine how best to move your work forward.

  Ultimately, as an entrepreneur, you control your destiny. Nobody else gets to dictate how you spend your time. Similarly, your life is not controlled by somebody else's agenda. When you're an entrepreneur, you control your time and you decide what you build with that time.

- **Ability to implement your ideas** – Most of us can remember a time at work (and it probably doesn't require long-term memory) when our ideas were shot down. True, many ideas are not really worth bringing to the table. But when you're working for somebody else, even good ideas struggle to take off. In most corporations, a promising idea must travel such a long journey up and down the chain of command that any promising signs of life are killed before anything happens.

All of this is entirely different when you're an entrepreneur. Running your own business gives you the freedom to experiment and implement an idea before determining its value. Obviously, the majority of ideas won't be that great, but in many cases, the best ideas come out of the process of playing around and testing things out.

In fact, the world's greatest ideas are very often the ones that at first appear to be a little bit nuts—the kind of ideas that would typically be shot down in a larger corporate setting. Venture capitalist Mark Andreessen, of Andreessen Horowitz, said, "It's very hard to make money on . . . consensus. Because if something is already consensus then money will have already flooded in and the profit opportunity is gone. And so by definition in venture capital, if you are doing it right, you are continuously investing in things that are non-consensus at the time of investment. And let me translate 'non-consensus': in sort of practical terms, it translates to crazy. You are investing in things that look like they are just nuts."[8]

Your crazy ideas may never see the light of day in the corporate realm. But in your own business, you can implement your ideas and wear "crazy" as a badge of honor.

- **Opportunity to take non-traditional paths** – Legend has it that the streets of Boston were originally built on long and winding cow paths, rather than the more traditional grid design used in places like New York City. On the surface, the twisting, non-traditional roads of Boston don't seem very sensible. But they give the city a unique style and look, and produce some of its best, most scenic views.

  The same can be said of entrepreneurship. The path you take as an entrepreneur will in many ways be non-traditional—but that's the beauty of it. Non-traditional paths, the ones not traveled by everybody else, are where you make discoveries. Being non-traditional makes you unique, and in business, uniqueness is very often what gives a company the differentiators needed to separate from the competition and succeed. Pursuing non-traditional paths is what being an entrepreneur is all about. These are the paths that lead to some of life's greatest opportunities.

- **Make a difference every day** – A number of years ago, I was an ecclesiastical leader for a congregation of roughly 200 young adults, many of whom I got to know very well. I was always impressed by the way many of them wanted to make a constant, ongoing difference in the world around them, rather than a single, one-off act of service. Rather than develop a scholarship fund at the end of their careers when they might have surplus money stashed away, they wanted to be directly involved in making a difference every day, starting right now.

As I will discuss in later chapters, becoming an entrepreneur and the desire to make a difference go hand in hand. In order to be successful, your business ventures must be built on something greater than just trying to make a lot of money. Profits are important, but at the end of the day, they're not enough alone to sustain the effort required to succeed in life and in business. That's why one of the defining features of authentically successful entrepreneurs is that they build ways of giving back directly into their businesses. This is, in fact, a key part of achieving true livelihood.

Of course, you don't have to be an entrepreneur to give back and make a difference. But running your own business opens up one-of-a-kind opportunities to serve those around you.

- **Break artificial restraints** – When I was feeling so frustrated by the job I described in Chapter 1, my wife told me I was like a horse with blinders on. Blinders don't actually "blind" a horse. Instead, they limit the horse's unique 180-degree vision, restricting it to roughly 30 degrees instead. In the company I was working for, it was much the same, as information was given out on a need-to-know basis only. Essentially, we were all forced to wear blinders and it was impossible to see the larger vision for what we were doing every day.

Becoming an entrepreneur is a guaranteed way to take off the blinders—and keep them off. When you are an entrepreneur, you never have to limit the scope of your vision. You get to decide your goals and aspirations. You define both what the "big picture" is and how you will make it a reality.

I've noticed that many Millennials desire—even require—a full vision of the organizations to which they belong. They want to know exactly what their efforts are helping to build. Entrepreneurship provides precisely this type of transparency and independence.

- **Build your professional life around your personal values** – One of the key concepts my colleagues and I teach in Launching Leaders is the need to consistently live the same set of values in all aspects of life. Unfortunately, our culture—and especially the corporate world—has adopted the idea that it's perfectly natural for people to live a compartmentalized life in which they follow one set of values at home and another at work. This runs against our innate humanness and makes it impossible to cultivate inner peace.

Counter to this trend, I've found that many Millennials place high value on authenticity. It is impossible to be authentic when you're constantly changing your moral compass. If you want a life of consistency and authenticity, becoming an entrepreneur allows you to build your professional life directly around your personal values. Ultimately, you can build an entire company geared toward actualizing your most important values.

Reasons Not to Become an Entrepreneur

- **You don't have the stomach for risk** – No matter what field or niche a business operates within, becoming an entrepreneur is defined by risk. In fact, I define true entrepreneurs as the ones with the most skin in the game, the ones who literally risk it all. An entrepreneur is the person who puts it all on the line—cash, time, and resources—to start a business, not the person who joins somebody else's team to avoid the risk. An entrepreneur is the person who sacrifices all other forms of income to focus 100% on growing their business, not the person who keeps a full-time job and tries to start something else "on the side."

As you consider becoming an entrepreneur, ask yourself if you can stomach the risk. As a Millennial, you already have a leg up when it comes to living with risk. Millennials have made an art of living on less and finding ways to survive in rough economic times. Still, not everyone is equipped to deal with the high levels of risk entrepreneurs must accept.

If the thought of taking huge risks to pursue your dreams is exciting, or if you're thrilled by the prospects of risking a lot in exchange for potentially huge rewards, then you're built for the entrepreneur's life. On the other hand, if the idea of risking everything keeps you up at night or makes you queasy, then don't push it. Be at peace with yourself and don't sweat it if you decide that entrepreneurship is not for you.

In some cases, you may feel your heart insisting that you're an entrepreneur, but you can't seem to get your mind and stomach to agree. If this happens, don't worry. You may never fully overcome the anxieties surrounding risk, but if you're willing to go for it despite your fears, you can certainly learn to manage them.

- **Working for someone else brings you peace and security** – As you try to sort out whether or not to become an entrepreneur, try to determine what "security" means to you. If you yearn to be in business for yourself and you find security in the possibility of being your own boss, then entrepreneurship could be the path for you. If, on the other hand, you believe that security is best achieved working for someone else, then you should be at peace with that and commit yourself to making a difference in that path. Remember, both the entrepreneur and the employee are respectable and needed. Neither one is a "sucker's choice." It's all about finding what's best for you.

Conclusion

If, after reading through everything in this chapter, the thought of setting out on your own burns in your heart and mind, filling you with an undeniable sense of excitement, then you likely have the entrepreneurial itch. This book will give you the skills and knowledge you need to bring relief to that itch.

And as for CJ: He chose not to go after the defense contractor job. In fact, almost immediately after making it to Laguna Beach he turned around and went to Tennessee. He recently told me that this is a stopping-off point as he considers his next adventure. He also said this current stop is giving him great autonomy over his schedule and time while also giving him the independence he needs to build important financial skills and personal resources. Whatever happens next, CJ is working out his plans for the entrepreneurial life—the Millennial way.

Chapter Summary

- Being an entrepreneur and being an employee for somebody else are equally valid, meaningful, and important. What matters is figuring out the best fit for you as a unique individual.

- As you consider what's best for you, weigh carefully all the points outlined in this chapter. Your path to fulfillment and happiness may not include becoming an entrepreneur—and that's OK.

- If you decide to pursue the entrepreneur's life, dive in, implement the ideas in this book, and never look back!

Invest In Yourself First: 8 Keys For Building A Strong Foundation

"Give me six hours to chop down a tree and I'll spend the first four sharpening the axe."

—Abraham Lincoln[9]

My father worked for the same company for 55 years before retiring comfortably. For better or worse, this traditional career path does not really exist anymore, which means you can no longer bank on finding one job that will carry you through your entire professional career and into retirement. Now, instead of focusing on landing that one golden job, you must create your own individual future by constantly expanding your knowledge, improving your skills, and discovering new ways to make yourself marketable.

As with so many other factors, the economic world in which you live—especially the changing job market—presents a number of unique challenges. But if you look at it the right way, this can also help prepare you for life as an entrepreneur. To thrive in today's economy, you must constantly improve and develop yourself, and that's exactly what it takes to successfully start your own business. The way I look at it, these efforts to improve, learn, and grow are really about investing in yourself. They're about establishing a foundation on which you can build for the rest of your life, professional and otherwise. Here are the eight most powerful ways to invest in yourself, thereby developing the tools you need to achieve your greatest goals.

Key #1: Practice Daily Mindfulness

I've always considered myself a deep thinker, and I've discovered that there is great power in taking time away from my busy schedule to quietly and privately perform what I call "Daily Mindfulness."

Daily Mindfulness is something you do every day to briefly separate yourself from the demands and routines of your busy life. The goal is to give yourself space to clear your mind, re-energize, and recalibrate toward your purpose and your most important values and goals.

What you actually do during your Daily Mindfulness is up to you since it should be a deeply personalized experience. Many people use their moments of Daily Mindfulness to study books that are sacred to them, pray, meditate, ponder, or simply be still and create a moment of peace. Think of it as a time to reflect on what you know, and to discover what you don't know. Whatever you do, the point is to carve out a period of time every day during which you check in with yourself and focus on the things that are most meaningful and important to you. As French scholar Pierre Hadot noted, "spiritual exercises" like the ones you pursue during Daily Mindfulness "provide a momentary stay against the stress and confusion of everyday life."[10]

Practicing Daily Mindfulness is necessary to discover your true path and direction. In fact, many of the most important answers and insights you'll discover in your life will take shape during your moments of Daily Mindfulness as you clear your heart and mind, and open yourself up to inspiration, revelation, insight, or whatever else you may call it.

Daily Mindfulness is how you channel your drive and passion toward the few things that truly matter, rather than having an orbit of junk circling your mind and cluttering your view. Ultimately, Daily Mindfulness empowers you to focus clearly so you can move ahead with confidence and enthusiasm.

Key #2: Define Your Purpose

Defining your purpose is a powerful and necessary way to invest in yourself before launching into the world of entrepreneurism. In fact, it is crucial if you want to live a holistic, authentic, and successful life. Your purpose will drive the decisions you make in all aspects of your life—including your entrepreneurial efforts. Remember, staying true to your core values and principles, regardless of where you are, what you're doing, or who you're with is essential for true success. Taking time to clearly define your purpose will give you something concrete to focus on and will make it easier to build this type of consistency into all aspects of your life.

Long before you hang the "open for business" sign out front, you must have a solid idea of how you want to change the world for the better. Your purpose establishes the specific way you intend to make a positive impact on those around you, on your professional field, and on the world in general. Of course, your purpose may evolve over time, but before such evolution and growth can occur, you must first have a solid starting place.

Defining your purpose requires some sustained introspection and soul searching, which is why Daily Mindfulness is a perfect time to begin this process. Similarly, if you're a spiritual or religious person, take time to study sacred texts, meditate, fast, and pray to gain insight into how you should best define your purpose. Ultimately, the goal is to define your purpose so concretely that you can write it down.[10]

Understand that I'm not talking about writing out a business plan. I'm talking about defining your more general purpose—the way you want to impact the world. In fact, don't even worry about any business-related specifics yet. Instead, use your purpose as a concrete goal to begin working toward right now, understanding that the fine-grained details will gradually come into focus along the way.

I call this process "painting with broad strokes." In Obliquity: Why Our Goals Are Best Achieved Indirectly, John Kay relates a powerful example of how painting with broad strokes works. According to Kay, pharmaceutical giant Johnson & Johnson was originally built around its purpose—provide real value to doctors, nurses, patients, mothers, fathers, and everyone else who needs health-related help—rather than on building a model to maximize profits. As the company set out to accomplish its purpose, the specific details of its business model naturally fell into place. As we all know, Johnson & Johnson went on to become one of the most successful businesses of all time.

To further illustrate how this process works, I'd like to share a story about the sustainable farm that my family and I operate. When we first purchased the farm, we dove right into trying to build a detailed business plan. But because this was new terrain for us, we quickly became overwhelmed trying to learn everything all at once, and we struggled to get anything off the ground. Finally, we stopped focusing on the details of our business model and instead went back to the basics. We defined our purpose:

> "We try to have as many plants and animals working together as possible to create a natural environment. As we do so, we have happier animals, create less waste, and produce more food per acre than any other type of farm. The animals and the land work in perfect harmony; the symbiotic relationship is palpable. Being good stewards of the animals and the earth is our passion."

With our purpose clearly defined, we suddenly had something concrete to work toward. Using my son-in-law's ingenious plans, we built our own chicken tractors, purchased 100 heritage chickens, and did everything we could to accomplish our purpose of providing these chickens a healthy, natural, sustainable habitat. We were soon harvesting and selling tons of all-natural eggs—and just like that, our business was underway. Since then, we've expanded to include not only chickens, but also pigs and grass-fed beef. Defining our purpose and painting with broad strokes catalyzed the entire thing. Having a clearly-defined purpose gave us something to work toward, and we learned what we needed along the way.

Key #3: Keep A Journal

As you define your purpose and begin working to make it a reality, write it all down in a journal. Keeping a journal helps you record the events of your life and track your progress toward your greatest purposes and goals.

Additionally, they help you articulate what is in your heart and mind. As you force yourself to write down what's going on in your life, things take on much more clarity and many times you'll end up learning things about yourself that you otherwise might have failed to see. To put it simply, journaling creates clarity and captures greatness.

A few years ago, I studied the lives of 15 of the greatest people who have ever lived. I noticed that journaling was one thing they all had in common. For example, Leonardo Da Vinci carried tiny pads of paper in his belt and whenever inspiration struck, he wrote it down. Through the course of his life, he created thousands of pages of illustrations, explanations, drawings, and writings. Nearly 7,000 pages of his notebooks still exist. Many of them include theories and sketches that were instrumental hundreds of years later when other people invented things like clocks, cars, bicycles, hydraulic equipment, and much more. Da Vinci's journals became powerful tools for documenting key moments of his life, exploring ideas, articulating important life values, concepts, and goals, and concretely tracking his progress toward them. They also ended up becoming invaluable to others many years later.

From what I've seen in my own experiences and in my studies of great people, journaling is a powerful tool, especially when combined with other keys outlined in this chapter, most notably, defining your purpose and engaging in Daily Mindfulness.

Key #4: Remember The 10,000 Hour Rule

In Outliers: The Story of Success, Malcolm Gladwell references a study in which scholars tracked a group of young music students from the time they first began learning to play an instrument, at around the age of five, until they were 20 years old.[12] Researchers found that the students who turned professional were the ones who put in at least 10,000 hours of practice. Based on this pattern, researchers concluded that the most important variable determining who would or would not excel was hard work—even more than "natural talent" or being "gifted."

Gladwell uses this and a number of similar studies and stories to argue that "the people at the very top don't work just harder or even much harder than everyone else. They work much, much harder."[13]

Ultimately, Gladwell formulates what has come to be known as "The 10,000 Hour Rule." This rule states that to become truly exceptional at any particular skill, a person must devote at least 10,000 hours to learning, practicing, and refining their craft. As neurologist Daniel Levitin puts it: "The emerging picture . . . is that ten thousand hours of practice is required to achieve the level of mastery associated with being a world-class expert—in anything."[14]

True success—the type of success I described earlier as true livelihood—isn't blind luck or pure happenstance; it is the outcome of lots of hard work. Anyone can become great, as long as they're willing to put in the hard work and time required to make it happen. The 10,000 Hour Rule also means that if you want to become great at something, you need to start learning, practicing, and developing your skills right now—and then stick with it for a lifetime.

In the midst of trying to reach the 10,000 hour mark you may have a brilliant idea for a new business. Should you wait to pursue this idea until you've put in your 10,000 hours? Not exactly. Many times, the process of learning, studying, and growing will inspire you with a great idea that could transform your life. When this happens, you have to act on your inspiration before the door of opportunity closes. You'll still need to hit the 10,000 hour mark to achieve true mastery, but most of your hours will come "on the job" as you figure things out along the way.

In fact, successful entrepreneurs often accrue their hours of training and preparation through a variety of different pathways, all of which work together to create a diverse and dynamic skill set. This may include formal schooling, past work experiences, on-the-fly learning as you launch a new company, and much more.

My son David's circuitous path toward entrepreneurism is an excellent example of this. His formal schooling culminated in a Master's degree in Peace and Conflict Resolution. While this may not at first appear to be directly related to entrepreneurism, the time and work he put into the degree actually made him uniquely qualified to become an excellent regional manager in our family business. Later, he decided to become an entrepreneur by entering the franchise world. As a franchisee, he was able to "borrow" the hours of work put in by others to develop a proven product and business model, but even this "borrowing" doesn't get him off the hook. He still needs to put in 10,000 hours of hard work, practice, and training to become a truly masterful business owner. The time and effort he's put into each of his various pursuits have certainly moved him closer to that goal, but mastery requires a lifetime of committed effort.

No matter where or how you put in your hours, the main point is that there are no shortcuts to success. You must devote 10,000 hours to your craft before you can become a master. You can't fake it, steal it, or masquerade as if you have it. Greatness comes only to those willing to work hard over an extended period of time. So get started now and stick with it.

Key #5: Get All the Education You Can

I was once speaking with a man who happened to be the CEO of a company. During our conversation, I asked him if he'd recently read any meaningful business books. He told me that he'd already reached the peak of his career and that he didn't need to waste his time reading business books anymore. I was shocked. On average, I read a book every two weeks, and I benefit immensely from striving to be a lifelong learner. In fact, it's because I put so much effort into reading that I'm able to stay active in a wide range of projects, from banking to farming to teaching, and as you are witnessing right now, writing.

To put it simply: Education is the fountain of opportunity. If you prioritize learning as much as you can throughout your entire life, you'll never become stagnant. Getting all the education you can is the best way to grow, develop, and progress, whether in business or any other aspect of your life.

In particular, reading is one of the most direct and powerful ways to educate yourself. Fortunately, reading is a skill that can be developed. When I was younger, I barely squeaked through high school, getting by with as little reading as possible. Years later, Ginger introduced me to the beautiful world of reading great books. When I first started, I was a very slow reader, and it took me a whole year to plow through a couple of titles. But as books began introducing me to so many life-changing ideas, I became hooked. I started reading as much as I could, and my reading skills gradually improved. Today, I can now read multiple books a month and my retention is exponentially better.

Obviously, business books will be directly relevant to your entrepreneurism. But don't limit yourself. Read novels, autobiographies, history, religion, and anything else that is positive, uplifting, or beautiful. Read about the lives of great individuals, study as much as you can, and ask your mentors for a list of their favorite books.

There has never been a better time to become an avid, lifelong learner. There are so many ways to access information: along with regular print books there are e-books, blogs, podcasts, YouTube videos, Google searches, and so much more. Many top-ranking universities provide free online lectures and courses.

Take advantage of all these opportunities and get as much education as you can. When you put forth effort to learn, you drink straight from the fountain of opportunity, ensuring that you will always be inspired, empowered, and consistently growing smarter. I can't think of a better way to invest in yourself.

Key #6: Adopt Great Mentors

Anytime I speak, write, or offer advice about entrepreneurial success, I always stress the importance of finding and adopting great mentors. Great mentors will help you refine and pursue your purpose and they will be an incredibly powerful source of lifelong learning as they share with you their knowledge and insights. I owe much of my success to the mentors I've had throughout my life, and now that I've successfully built several businesses of my own, I try to give back by mentoring other up-and-coming entrepreneurs.

Before you seek out mentors, you must have a strong sense of your purpose (see Key #2). What kind of person do you want to become? What sorts of things do you want to accomplish in your life? What are your primary objectives for starting a business? How will your business positively impact the world around you? The answers to these questions give you a rubric you can use to identify people who could be effective mentors.

From there, seek out successful individuals who have the expertise, skills, and experience that will help you accomplish your goals. Then, when you meet someone you think would be a good fit, ask them directly and politely if they would mentor you. Tell them a bit about yourself, your ideas, and your objectives, and be clear about what you are looking for in a mentor.

Finally, remember that mentoring is a two-way street. You can't simply leach off your mentors. You should also look for ways to give back to them. Be mindful of what your mentors do for you and regularly take time to show them your appreciation. When you have a great mentor, the interactions you have with one another should lift both of you.[15]

Key #7: Let Time Work for You

There is a space between the moment you commit to becoming an entrepreneur and the day you actually open for business. This space is when you prepare for success. Too often, young startups go to launch without enough preparation and they end up becoming one of the 80% of all new businesses that fail in the first year. In many cases, these failures could have been avoided with a little patience and some additional planning. As a general guideline, I typically start with a viable business plan and then double the amount of time and startup capital initially estimated as necessary to achieve profitability. What you do during those years sets the tone for success or failure.

After Ginger and I made the commitment to become entrepreneurs, we worked with our mentor and accountant to develop a five-year financial plan. We then formalized our commitment to this plan by typing it up and signing it.

Our plan was geared around letting time work for us. We committed to eliminating unnecessary expenses, taking no new loans, making no credit card purchases, and limiting ourselves to very few new clothes and inexpensive dating, eating, and entertainment. At the same time, we began growing a little nest egg by devoting a predetermined portion of our income to a savings account. As that account grew, we used it to make strategic investments to accelerate the growth of our savings.

Even though we were only putting a relatively small amount of money into that account each month, after five years of strictly following this plan, we had enough set aside to launch our business with some degree of financial security. During those years, we were also able to study and make strategic plans that set us up for a successful launch. All in all, these years of preparation enabled us to harness the power of time, using it to build a strong foundation. We realized early on that those preparatory years of hard work and discipline would produce much bigger results down the road—and that's exactly what happened.[16]

Key #8: Build a Reserve of Cash

My wife's grandparents were incredible people, and Ginger and I had the pleasure of visiting with them often during the early years of our marriage. We would play cards or board games together, cook with them, and even make sausage. During this time, Grandpa and Grandma shared some great wisdom with us.

In particular, they shared a powerful financial insight. Grandpa was in business for himself as an electrician and locksmith, and although he and Grandma never seemed have much money, they were never in debt and they always managed to have more than sufficient for their needs. They weren't millionaires, but they clearly knew how to handle their finances. One of Grandpa's favorite sayings was "cash is king." I didn't understand what this meant at first, but I eventually grew to appreciate what he was trying to tell us: Save your money to give yourself financial stability.

For up-and-coming entrepreneurs, this concept means building up a cash reserve on which a young company can begin to grow. Obviously, this requires financial discipline, but if you're working to harness the power of time as outlined in Key #7, then you're already moving in this direction.

Building a cash reserve is crucial because it enables your company to weather the financial ups and downs that define the early years of a startup. Furthermore, a cash reserve often becomes the key to unlocking the additional capital needed to give your company legs. Many investors are only interested in backing entrepreneurs who are willing to put their own funds on the line. For example, when I judge business competitions at universities, or when I consider a real-world investment opportunity, this is exactly what I look for. I am only interested in entrepreneurs who are willing to put up at least half of the capital needed to get things started. This demonstrates determination and grit, and shows that they have real skin in the game.

The same is true of most banks. It's standard practice for banks to expect entrepreneurs to front at least 25% of the amount they're asking for in a loan, as well as provide sufficient collateral in case the new business flops and the loan defaults.

Obviously, it takes time to establish the financial wherewithal to build up a cash reserve, but living with discipline, planning effectively, and letting time work to your benefit will enable you to build the cash reserve required to earn the trust of others and to give yourself a secure foundation.

The bottom line: Cash is king (or queen)!

One Last Thought

As you begin implementing these eight principles into your life, remember that we are all works in progress. Don't expect instant perfection or immediate results. The point is to establish meaningful and empowering long-term habits.

I can personally confirm that the concepts outlined in this chapter take a lifetime to master; I'm still working at them. But I can also say that empowerment comes through the effort itself. The work you put into making these principles part of your daily life will build the foundation you need for success, both as an entrepreneur and as a person. Be patient with yourself and enjoy the growth you experience throughout the journey.

Chapter Summary

- Entrepreneurial success starts by investing in yourself. This is how you build a strong foundation for the rest of your life.

- Focus on these eight keys for investing in yourself:

  1. Practice Daily Mindfulness.

  2. Define your purpose and make it the driving force behind everything you do.

  3. Keep a journal to document your life and learn about yourself.

  4. True mastery comes through The 10,000 Hour Rule" —start working now!

  5. Decide to be a lifelong learner.

  6. Seek out and adopt mentors who are a good fit for you and your life goals.

  7. Harness the power of time by being disciplined with your finances.

  8. Cash is king (or queen!)—invest in yourself and your future by saving now.

The Mindset of Money

"I just want enough money not to have to calculate."

—Dietrich Bonnhoeffer[17]

Purpose Before Profits

In the last chapter, my second key for investing in yourself was taking time to concretely and carefully define your purpose. This is a crucial step because once you establish your purpose—which can also be thought of as your calling or your passion—you give yourself something concrete on which to focus your entrepreneurial efforts. Of course, defining your purpose doesn't magically spell out all the fine-grained business details for you. Instead, focusing on your purpose allows you to immediately set out toward a clear objective, painting with broad strokes and allowing the more specific details to come into focus along the way.

There are any number of possible purposes that may motivate a person to start a business, but the key is trying to articulate in writing the specific reasons you think your business ideas will make a difference, change the world for the better, or help you build a foundation for moving forward through life.

It's important that you think about your purpose in terms of the impact you want to make. If your purpose is primarily about making more money, your endeavors will be as empty as your bank account. But if your efforts are motivated by a larger purpose, you will always have something powerful driving you, something that transcends the ups and downs of the market, the temporary financial struggles your business may face, or any other negatives. Ironically, your bank account will probably grow as well.

I'm not saying that making a profit isn't important; it's actually critical. I'm saying that the purpose behind the profits is the engine that drives successful businesses. Focusing on how your entrepreneurship will make a positive difference in the world is what will cause your business to blossom and flower into a beautiful bouquet. "People over profits" is a good motto to embrace.

In Obliquity, John Kay describes the incredible success of Boeing. According to Kay, Boeing's first CEO, Bill Allen (from 1945-1968), pushed the company to focus on its purpose, which he defined as "eat, breathe, and sleep the world of aeronautics."[18] With this purpose in mind, the company began building airplanes out of the employees' collective love of aviation.

Interestingly, because the company focused primarily on its purpose and its passion, it quickly established a reputation for building some of the world's best, most innovative aircraft. This naturally drove incredible profits and Boeing eventually went on to become one of the biggest names in the aeronautics industry. The company's huge success didn't come from a love of profits, but from a love of airplanes.

Again, I'm not saying that profits aren't important. I'm saying that you must have purpose and passion first. When your purpose drives your efforts, you will naturally push for greatness, the profits will start rolling in, and as they do, they will mean much more to you than mere dollars and cents.

Guy Kawasaki articulates this by explaining that it's more important to "make meaning" than it is to make money.

In The Art of the Start, he writes: "Meaning is not about money, power, or prestige. It's not even about creating a fun place to work. Among the meanings of 'meaning' are to:

- Make the world a better place;
- Increase the quality of life;
- Right a terrible wrong;
- Prevent the end of something good."[19]

Your purpose needs to be at the center of everything you do, and it must become the heartbeat of your entrepreneurial efforts. Your purpose must also be the foundation on which you build a healthy mindset toward money.

Change Your Mindset

Assuming you've established your purpose, it's now time to talk about money. Although profits should not be the main focus of what you do, you must nonetheless ensure that your ideas and efforts make money. An unprofitable venture does nothing to advance your long-term purpose and going out of business doesn't align with anybody's core values. Establishing a healthy mindset toward money is how you move from pursuing your purpose to actually realizing that purpose.

In society, we are inundated by ideas about money, and this has a profound effect on how we think about and approach this subject. Many of these ideas have been around for generations, and can be summarized in a few well-known idioms that you're probably familiar with:

- Money doesn't grow on trees.
- We can't afford it.
- Use it up, wear it out, make it do or do without.
- Money can't buy happiness.

These phrases, and the beliefs behind them, come out of very particular time periods. For example, my parents believed in each of these maxims and they both grew up through the Great Depression, an experience that forged their mindsets toward money. They never took any amount of money for granted, and their frugal approach allowed them to achieve some pretty impressive results: they bought cars with cash, lived without credit cards, they successfully provided for all five of their kids, and after making a steady wage working for the same company for 55 years, my father retired with enough cash saved up for him and my mother to live comfortably.

Throughout their life together, my parents never had tons of money, and although we never lived a fancy lifestyle or took long and exotic vacations, none of us went without. My parents always had enough for their needs plus a little extra, and they always lived in gratitude rather than a state of wanting more. Clearly, the mindset they developed toward money served them well, in large part because it was tailored to the specific time in which they lived. Back when my dad was building his career, the go-to-work escalator maintained steady upward momentum, which allowed him to provide for himself and his family.

But the world today is very different, and while my parents' mindset toward money worked when they were in their 20s and 30s, it may not be as relevant to your situation. The financial context in which most folks in the rising generations have grown up is characterized by high educational costs, student debt, employment challenges, wage stagnation, and exaggerated views of what wealth looks like on social media. In many cases, dealing with difficulties like student debt and a poor job market leads to other problems such as credit card debt, which compounds an already-stressful situation.

Even so, learning to survive all this has made you and your generation more likely to succeed in the entrepreneurial world. Millennials have figured out how to develop their own security nets and build their own networks to guide and protect their financial futures. For example, Millennials participate in crowdfunding campaigns three times more frequently than Baby Boomers and 70% more frequently than Generation Xers; 59% of all Millennials say they save; and over 50% do their banking online, choosing to forego traditional, face-to-face interactions with bank tellers.[20] In other words, you and Millennials like you are blazing your own financial trails, using your own tools, ideas, resources, and communities to do it.

This is precisely the type of resourcefulness, creativity, and determination required to succeed as an entrepreneur.[21] It's also proof that a fundamental shift is happening in how your generation thinks about money. In many ways, the mindsets that worked for your parents and grandparents are giving way to new mindsets. The old approaches to money were based on protecting what a person earned and tended to view money in terms of scarcity. Today, the new generations are learning to cultivate different mindsets that are more open to taking calculated risks, coming up with creative ways to access resources, and that tend to see money as a tool for achieving larger life goals. Don't discard the previous generations' mindsets regarding money; just be sure to refine and tailor these lessons to make them relevant to your own experience.

In order to cultivate a healthy mindset toward money that can keep up with today's rapidly-changing economy, you must adjust your approach and your thinking. You can't get stagnant. Your mindset must be proactive and flexible. If you haven't already, it's time to change your mindset away from the old assumptions of previous generations and adopt instead a more dynamic mindset toward money.

Cultivate an Attitude of Abundance

The key to all this is cultivating what I call an "attitude of abundance." Let me give you an example of this concept from my own life.

When I retired, I suddenly found myself needing to adjust my mindset toward money. Things changed dramatically when I stepped off the speedy hamster wheel of running a large company and climbed onto the slow-moving canoe of retirement. From a financial perspective, the biggest change was no longer receiving steady paychecks. Don't get me wrong, I had plenty of cash saved up, but my mindset automatically placed focus on what I no longer had rather than on what I could have in my new life. My mindset slipped into one of fear, protectiveness, and scarcity instead of an attitude of abundance.

One day, I went grocery shopping with Ginger. Standing in line to check out, I thought about how all the other people in the store had jobs, paychecks, and livelihoods, and were now running around getting the things they needed to survive and be happy. I felt intense anxiety since I was no longer one of these people bringing in a steady paycheck.

I looked into my cart and instinctively put my box of Cap'n Crunch back on the shelf, telling myself it was a luxury I could no longer afford. Ginger saw this and quickly put the cereal back in our shopping cart.

She began coaching me, reminding me that although we had sold our company, we hadn't retired from life. With her help, I realized that I needed to change my mindset toward money. I gradually began moving my mindset away from an attitude of fear and toward an attitude of abundance. Here are some of the specific thoughts and assumptions I needed to shift:

Attitude of Fear	Attitude of Abundance
You are retired and poor.	You are not retired from the rest of the things that are meaningful to you and you have more than sufficient for your needs.
You don't have a regular paycheck.	Your paydays, although irregular, are more than enough for what you need at this point. More importantly, you worked incredibly hard preparing for this time of your life—enjoy it!
You will wither and die without the job and the paychecks you were used to.	I will make each day a new day of adventure and I will strive to make a meaningful contribution every day.
You can no longer afford Cap'n Crunch.	Cap'n Crunch is one of the food groups, so load up!

I'm telling you this story to highlight a couple key points. First, it's important to develop a dynamic mindset toward money that can adapt and evolve. This includes moving beyond outdated ideas as well as changing your mindset to meet the specific, constantly-changing circumstances of your life. When I was your age, I had to develop a new mindset toward money that would allow me to become a successful entrepreneur. In my later years, I needed to change my mindset again to accommodate my new situation.

Second, this story illustrates what it means to have an attitude of abundance. Instead of focusing on all the things I didn't have, all the things I thought I couldn't afford, and all the things I thought I could no longer have in my life, I needed to focus on what I did have, what I could afford, and all the new things I could do with my life. I needed to change my mindset from fear to abundance.

This same concept applies directly to entrepreneurship. Ginger and I achieved our best periods of growth, success, and profitability when we tried to cultivate an attitude of abundance. We stopped viewing our funds as scarce resources that needed to be carefully protected and began seeing them as tools for even greater growth. We invested in more business ventures and became more willing to take on smart risks in order to build on what we already had.

I'm not suggesting that you take unnecessary risks or make frivolous decisions. I'm suggesting that to succeed as an entrepreneur, you need to change your mindset toward money by cultivating an attitude of abundance. When you shift your thinking and begin focusing on what you already have—rather than what you don't yet have—and when you begin seeing your money and other assets as tools for achieving your greater purpose, you will be amazed at how much you can achieve and how much more meaningful your successes will become.

Reframing the Myths of Money

When you approach money with an attitude of abundance you allow yourself to see through the negative myths about money that still define how many of us think. But building a healthy mindset toward money isn't just about replacing negative thoughts with positive ones. It's about fundamentally reshaping your views in a way that facilitates—rather than inhibits—your ability to succeed.

Here are some of the most dangerous myths that still dominate how our society thinks about money, followed up by some suggestions for how to reframe them in much more positive and productive ways.

You can't be rich and spiritual. Many of us grow up in religions, cultures, and societies that view wealth as inherently and fundamentally opposed to the ideals of a humble, community-oriented, serving, and spiritual lifestyle.

Fortunately, this myth is simply not true. In fact, one of the key concepts we teach in Launching Leaders is that people can lead honest, upright, service-oriented, and spiritual lives while still setting themselves up to follow their entrepreneurial dreams—which can also include becoming wealthy.

As my colleagues and I have taught this principle, we've seen people around the world create and expand brand new opportunities for themselves without diminishing their spirituality. In fact, adopting a more positive approach to making money has set them free to give back, serve, and control their destinies in ways they wouldn't have been able to otherwise. Money creates new and unique chances to serve others and make a positive impact on the world around you.

Reframe the myth "you can't be rich and spiritual" to "wealth will empower me to magnify my spiritual ambitions."

Money can't buy happiness. The heck it can't. With the exception of simply spending time with loved ones, there are few things I love doing that don't require money. Whether it's fly fishing, farming, traveling, or even reading, they all require money.

We've all heard the saying that "money isn't evil, the love of money is." I'm here to say that money is good if it is used as the fuel that allows you to do good. In fact, there are a lot of really incredible acts of service that can dramatically change the world that require money—and in many cases, lots of it.

Whether you're trying to pursue the things in life that bring you joy or you're trying to serve others, the amount of money you need to be happy is totally subjective. But make no mistake about it: you gotta have cheddar.

Reframe the myth "money can't buy happiness" to "money supports my happiness."

The Last Word

Talking about money is not an easy conversation. Most folks like to keep their financial cards close to their chest, but this is beginning to change as 20- and 30-somethings insist on more authentic, transparent relationships and conversations. One of the reasons it's often so difficult or awkward to talk about money is because the ideas we've been raised with tend to frame money in negative ways that make it look like having money inherently contradicts the values of selflessness, love, service, and working to create a better world. But these are unproductive and largely untrue myths.

The fact is that money, in one form or another, plays a huge part in our everyday lives. The lights don't work without money. The roads aren't maintained without money. We need money to brush our teeth, wash our clothes, or watch TV. There are few things we do in life that are not connected in some way to money.

Rather than being afraid of money or clinging to reductive myths, the trick is cultivating a healthy mindset toward money. Rather than viewing money through the negative lenses of fear, scarcity, and selfishness, change your mindset so that you see money as a positive resource for pursuing your purpose and achieving your life goals.

Be grateful for the money you have, for the chance you have to make money, and for the service opportunities money makes possible. Become a good steward of money and use it to build an abundant life aimed at pursuing the things that make you truly happy, while also finding new ways to make a positive impact.

I invite you to consider your own mindset toward money and reframe it whenever necessary. Doing so will help you advance your purpose and enjoy life. So go ahead, put the Cap'n Crunch back in your cart and live with an attitude of abundance.

Chapter Summary

- Define your purpose before worrying about money; "people before profits" is a good starting place.

- Profits are a key aspect of being an entrepreneur—without making money you can't stay in business and you can't advance your purpose.

- Change your mindset toward money by abandoning outdated beliefs and tailoring your mindset to meet your specific life circumstances.

- Cultivate an attitude of abundance by focusing on what you have and what you can do, rather than stressing about what you don't have or what you think you can't do.

- Reframe negative myths about money to facilitate—rather than inhibit—success.

Leap! It's Now or Never

―――

"The only impossible journey is the one you never begin."

―Tony Robbins[22]

In 2010, Ginger and I traveled to New Zealand for a Launching Leaders conference. We took our daughter, Lexie, with us. Lexie had just left the university where she'd been studying and was at a crossroads in her life, working to shift her mindset and figure out what to pursue next. In the midst of these changes, she wasn't the most confident in herself, although she remained strong in her sense of personal identity.

During this trip, entirely out of the blue, she asked me: "Hey Dad, wanna bungee jump with me?" She knew we were in one of the most iconic locations for bungee jumping anywhere in the world and she'd apparently gotten the idea to give it a shot. "Sure?" I answered in a wavering voice.

A short time later, I found myself at the bottom of the Auckland Bridge, getting strapped in to a harness. Step by step we got a little bit closer to the top of the bridge, and step by step my stomach grew a little queasier. My palms started sweating. I was a skilled pilot and was used to heights, but I'd never considered doing anything like this.

Lexie was a few steps ahead of me and before I knew it, we were standing on the platform at the pinnacle of the bridge. It was decision time. Lexie had already made up her mind and she was fully committed to this crazy adventure.

I, on the other hand, was still considering my options and thinking through my doubts. Was my estate plan in place? What if the bungee mechanism wasn't measured properly and I was about to dive a few hundred feet into the ocean abyss? At the last moment, I decided not to jump. I told myself I'd

document Lexie's bravery by writing about it instead, and I stepped back to watch. Her jump was magnificent. The bungees perfectly slowed her

 descent, letting her dip into the ocean to the depth of her waist before catapulting her back into the air. We have pictures and videos of her jump, which proved to be life changing. Her leap became the door to a new life of adventure and meaning. From that point on, she began making decisions that set her on a path to new experiences and possibilities she'd never considered before, and she began traveling those paths with confidence and faith.

This photo says it all. You can see the excitement in her face, not only for having completed an incredible adventure, but also for the exhilarating sense of committing to new paths in life. As for me, I was thrilled to share this moment of celebration with my daughter, and although I regret not taking the leap myself, I think it was even more empowering for her to experience the adventure on her own.

I've thought a lot about Lexie's experience that day, and I think it's the perfect analogy for becoming an entrepreneur. Like bungee jumping, starting your own business is an adventure full of great risk and even greater reward. Similarly, the only way to experience the thrill of success is to do what Lexie did: make a decision, commit yourself, go with your gut, and take the leap!

5 Principles for a Successful Launch

Using Lexie's experience as a starting place, I'd like to outline four principles that will guide you toward a successful launch.

1. Prepare for launch, but don't analyze your cuticles. Before Lexie could successfully complete her jump, she needed to prepare by putting on her harness, hiking to the top of the bridge, and then getting strapped to the bungee cord. These preparations were absolutely necessary, but if she had taken too long, over-analyzed her decision, or let herself become indecisive and doubtful, this brief period of preparation could have turned into an obstacle keeping her from making the leap. That's essentially the trap I fell into that day.

Entrepreneurism is very much the same. You must prepare as much as you can, make the ascent to launch, and secure for yourself some sort of bungee cord that will keep you from crashing and drowning. That's what you're doing when you invest in yourself, adopt great mentors, define your purpose, and implement the principles you're learning in this book.

As with bungee jumping, there's no way your entrepreneurial adventure will succeed without these preparations, but you also can't sit around so long that preparing becomes a roadblock. I've known many "wannabe" entrepreneurs who get stuck in the rut of preparing and analyzing so much that either their great idea is taken up by someone else or they simply never get around to launching their business.

Chapter 3 talks about defining your purpose and then moving forward with broad strokes, trusting that the finer details will follow. When you adopt this approach, you prepare yourself for success without getting so bogged down that you miss out on the adventure of leaping toward your dreams.

2. Leap with an attitude to risk it all. Even after preparing and building safety mechanisms for yourself, entrepreneurism is defined by risk. Make no mistake about it, in order to succeed you must embrace this risk and go all in.

This is exactly how bungee jumping works. Although the risk of dying while bungee jumping is a tiny 1:500,000 there is still a chance that a bungee jumper could lose it all. Lexie knew this, but she didn't let it stop her. She made up her mind, completed the necessary preparations, and without wasting any time, leaped off the Auckland Bridge toward the ocean below—how cool is that! In your startup, it's important to understand the risks involved, but don't let them scare you off. Instead, recognize your reality and launch with confidence, trust, and an attitude to risk it all.

3. Leave the comforts of home. I use this phrase figuratively, recognizing that many 20- and 30-somethings live at home for very real and legitimate economic reasons. What I'm really driving at is that in order to have a successful launch, you must be willing to leave behind certain comforts. This is part of launching with an attitude to risk it all. The bootstrap years require big-time sacrifices but instead of seeing this as a negative, look at it as simply another part of the fun and exciting journey of entrepreneurism.

4. Embrace vulnerability. Vulnerability is a very familiar experience for entrepreneurs—especially during the early stages. When you're trying to launch a new idea, business, or product, you are sharing with the world an extremely important and intimate part of yourself, your life, and your passion. You are sharing with others the thing you devoted endless hours of study, preparation, and hard work to grow and develop, and when you go out on a limb like that, you make yourself vulnerable to ridicule, embarrassment, financial loss, and failure.

Feeling vulnerable can sometimes be so uncomfortable that people end up doing whatever they can to avoid anything that makes them feel that way. But, as social researcher and best-selling author Brené Brown argues, we should not avoid vulnerability, we should embrace it.

She writes: "Vulnerability is not weakness, and the uncertainty, risk, and emotional exposure we face every day are not optional. . . . Our willingness to own and engage with our vulnerability determines the depth of our courage and the clarity of our purpose; the level to which we protect ourselves from being vulnerable is a measure of our fear and disconnection."[23]

By definition, being an entrepreneur carries many risks, and when you hang the "open for business" sign on the front door, you are making yourself vulnerable to these risks. Failure happens, and when it does it hurts. But this is not a reason to avoid playing the game. In fact, according to Brown, embracing vulnerability is a deeply empowering way to grow as a person—and, as I'm suggesting, as an entrepreneur as well.

In your life as an entrepreneur, don't run from your vulnerabilities. Instead, recognize that feeling vulnerable is an unavoidable part of the entrepreneurial path and embrace this experience as a necessary part of the journey. When you find yourself feeling vulnerable, use it as a chance to face your fears, practice humility, learn about yourself, and grow.

5. Be your own ant. I've always been fascinated by ants. When I was a kid, I loved putting them in a glass aquarium and watching them work. Now, as an adult, the more I study and learn about them the more intrigued I become.

Ants are incredibly powerful, capable of lifting objects more than 20 times their own body weight. They "absorb" the world around them, "hearing" vibrations in their feet and "breathing" through tiny holes all over their bodies. Ants are also fierce, to the point that when they fight it's usually to the death. On top of all this, ants are deeply committed to their communities, with some ant colonies covering more than 3,000 miles—that's a massive social network, all without the use of Facebook!

In many ways, 20- and 30-somethings share many similarities with ants. Millennials have a keen and intuitive way of "sensing" the world around them, they tend to be very social (especially on social media), and they fight hard for the things they believe in. There are also many connections between ants and successful entrepreneurs, since to succeed in the business world you have to be tenacious, good at collaborating with others, committed to your purpose, and unrelenting in your pursuit of greatness.

I use the phrase "be your own ant" because I want you to emulate all of the best, most productive qualities of ants, and then do something very un-ant-like: leave behind the hierarchical colony and be your own ant. This doesn't mean going it alone. You'll have your mentors, the team you build as your business grows, and other sources of insight and knowledge (like this book) to guide you. Entrepreneurism requires the relentless hard work and resolute determination of an ant, coupled with a strong commitment to your unique individuality. Be your own ant!

Caution: Turbulence Ahead

Each of these principles is crucial for a successful launch. But they don't mean that your launch will be easy or pain-free. In fact, difficulties will definitely arise, which is why we now need to talk about how to deal with the challenges of launching a startup.

If you've ever heard a pilot say "turbulence ahead" you know the feeling of tensing up and bracing for the worst. As a pilot, I never really know exactly when turbulence will occur, I just know that it will. This is exactly the attitude you should have when you launch a business. Although you won't be able to predict when challenges will arise, know that they will and be prepared to meet them.

When I started my first company, a key part of my preparation was putting in the due diligence with attorneys to ensure that any non-compete agreements from my previous job did not apply to my new business. After confirming that there was no way my new company violated previous agreements, I opened the doors and launched.

Even though I made sure I was legally in the clear, within a few months of launch, my former employer filed a lawsuit against me. While the case was pending, I was barred from operating in southern California, which unfortunately was my primary market at the time.

This created severe turbulence for the entire company—and it dragged on for seven long years. The turmoil I experienced during this challenging time led me to the darkest point of my life and I found myself doubting everything. At my lowest, I sat huddled in the closet believing that God had abandoned me, and I found myself confronting suicidal thoughts. Fortunately, God had not given up on me, and my wife, family, and faith came to the rescue. They helped me weather the storm and together we pressed on.

Surprisingly, those years of extreme turbulence ultimately ended up catalyzing explosive growth that I could never have foreseen. Since we were forced to stop working in southern California, where my business was headquartered, we had to bump up our timeline and move into new states and new markets much quicker than I'd anticipated. By the time we finally settled the suit, my company was operating in several new states and we were in a much stronger position than when the drama first began.

I earnestly hope that nobody has to experience such severe turbulence, but as surely as the sun rises each morning, turbulence and challenges of some sort will come. When they do, remember that it's not necessarily because you messed up or failed. Turbulence is a natural part of the process as a new business unfolds, grows, changes, dips, dodges, and scores home runs—sometimes all in a single month!

Viewing turbulence as a natural and unavoidable part of being an entrepreneur helps you approach these experiences as opportunities to learn, grow, and figure out how to maximize your strengths. During these moments, it may be helpful to remember that nothing in nature grows without facing obstacles. Seeds must overcome the resistance of the soil before they can break the crust and begin growing. Trees must survive the heavy burdens of snow and wind just as businesses—especially startups—must overcome the resistance of competition, market forces, and unforeseen challenges in order to succeed.

When you're in the middle of working through turbulence, it's easy to get down on yourself and convince yourself that you're a failure. But when you're feeling at your lowest, you're actually in extremely good company. For example, Walt Disney was fired from a newspaper for "lacking imagination" and having "no original ideas." Albert Einstein couldn't speak until he was almost four years old and his teachers said, "he will never amount to anything." When he was 30 years old, Steve Jobs was left devastated and depressed after being kicked out of the company he founded. The Beatles were rejected by Decca Recording Studios when producers said, "they have no future in show business."[24] And the list goes on and on. Everyone who starts something will inevitably face challenges before they blossom and grow.

One Final Thought

I have an artist friend who makes sculptures out of clay. Some artists work very fast and complete projects quickly, but my friend typically devotes around 200 hours to each individual piece. At the end of her painstaking work, she has to fire the clay in a kiln.

My friend is extremely nervous during this phase of the project because, as she explained to me, clay sometimes explodes while it fires. If the clay is too moist, the water turns to steam and exits the clay so quickly it takes out everything around it like a grenade.

Knowing this, whenever a sculpture finishes firing, and the kiln cools down from its peak 1,800 degrees, my friend nervously opens the top of the oven to see how it turned out. Sometimes she sees only shards, but more often, she sees the beautiful culmination of all those hours of hard work and dedication.

I suppose the best way for my friend to avoid the pain of having one of her pieces explode is to never create anything in the first place. That route is completely safe, and she can be 100% sure she will never have another sculpture explode. But obviously, this is a crazy thought. She loves her work and is committed to her craft, and she would never think of quitting just to avoid risk or pain. Yet how often do we prevent ourselves from doing things because we're afraid our plans might "blow up?" How often do we fail to make the leap because we let the possibility of failure overshadow the possibility of great success?

Avoiding risk altogether might technically be safer, but it will never allow you to achieve your dreams or become the person you were meant to be. So go ahead and take the leap. Create something beautiful, knowing full well that turbulence is ahead. There is no magic formula for calculating the precise time to launch your business, but if you're committed to your purpose, willing to work hard, and trying to be as prepared as you can, you'll know when it's time.

Chapter Summary

- When you know it's time to launch, take the leap!
- Keep in mind these five principles to achieve a successful launch:

    1. Prepare but don't over-analyze; start with broadstrokes and fill in the detail as you go.

    2. Leap with an attitude to risk it all.

    3. Leave the comforts of home and enjoy the sacrifices you make during the bootstrap years.

    4. Embrace vulnerability.

    5. Be your own ant.

- Know that challenges will come and embrace them as powerful opportunities to grow.

Draft Your Team and Protect the Mothership

"Great things in business are never done by one person. They're done by a team of people."

—Steve Jobs[25]

When Ginger and I decided to take the leap and start our first business, we didn't believe we could handle the risk all by ourselves. I talked to a friend I'd hired at my previous job and asked him to partner with us. He agreed and even though I knew the new business wasn't his true passion, Ginger and I felt we needed the moral support.

After one month of working 80-hour weeks, my friend told us he wasn't able to put in that much time, and that it was unfair for him to continue as a partner. This wasn't too surprising, since he was at a different stage of life than me and Ginger—he was older than us and had slightly different priorities. Additionally, he already had other side businesses of his own dividing his time. Remember the importance of going all in when you start a business? Ginger and I were fully committed, but he was stretched a little too thin.

Long story short: he was soon divested of his ownership and Ginger and I owned 100% of the business instead of half of it. This ended up being the best thing that ever happened to our little company, and I'm glad it happened early on and that the decision was mutual and amicable.

It's fairly common for young entrepreneurs to feel intimidated by the risks and challenges they are about to face, and to seek out someone who can share those burdens. Sometimes partnerships work out just fine, but before deciding too quickly to look for a partner, slow down and realize that you may simply be feeling anxious, worried, and lacking confidence—all of which are natural responses to setting out on such a big mission. Furthermore, before rushing out to find a partner, recognize that at some point you will need to hire people and build a team to help you run your business, which means you won't actually be alone after all. Building a strong team often ends up being more effective—and more profitable—than immediately rushing to form a full partnership with somebody.

In fact, drafting and building an all-star team is one of the most important keys to entrepreneurial success. At this point in the process, you should have already defined your purpose, adopted great mentors, invested in yourself, and taken the leap toward launching your own business. Now, as you work to give your young business legs to stand on, it's critical to understand that no one succeeds alone.

In Michael Gerber's book, The E-Myth Revisited, he teaches that entrepreneurial dreams will fall apart unless the entrepreneur recognizes early on the importance of assembling a solid team.[26] The reality is that very few entrepreneurs can transform their great idea, dream, or passion into a successful business all on their own. They need others on their team whose gifts and talents will complement theirs.

Regardless of how smart or talented you are, there will always be certain things you can't do or that you aren't good at, which is why accountants, legal, HR, marketing, production, technicians, managers, and so on are necessary to round out and complete your team. This chapter will outline the most important concepts and practices to follow as you begin assembling your team.

Don't Give Away the Gold

Stock in your new company is gold. It's what gives you the privileges of ownership, and more importantly, it's what gives you control of your destiny. Whatever approach you end up taking toward stock ownership, keep these principles in mind:

1. Never give up voting control.

If you end up in a three-way partnership, and each of you owns 33.3% of the company, you do not have control. Anytime the other shareholders can mass a majority of the vote, you've lost control of your company. Sadly, I've learned that when money or stock is on the line, people often act very differently than you would guess—even people you know well. Understanding this, it's best to separate out personal feelings and relationships and handle the issue of stock as a matter of objective business practice. Whatever you do, never give up voting control.

2. Never give away stock.

It's wise to recognize that you don't have all the talent you need to run your company. But don't let this realization make you so worried or desperate that you end up making rash decisions. Too often, young entrepreneurs panic when challenges arise and, in an attempt to keep the company moving forward, they start giving away part of the company to attract top-notch talent. Many times, employees may also try to use stocks as a bargaining chip. Don't fall into this trap. Do not entice talent with stock. Instead, in your negotiations with potential employees, leverage variables like salary, leadership, and opportunities for advancement.

Evaluate the Intangibles

At some point in your career you will probably run into an employee that we'll refer to as "Joe"—in fact, you may already know this sort of character. Joe can best be described by words like disloyal, disruptive, abrasive, self-absorbed, whiny, untrustworthy, unaware, and selfish.

One of the worst things you can do for your business is make accommodations for Joe. A team will eventually sink to the level of its worst player, and if you keep Joe around, your entire team will gradually lose enthusiasm and commitment, and the overall enjoyment of working together will disappear. I understand that you may have a desire to help Joe, or that you might hope that Joe will improve, and while these are admirable thoughts, hope is not a strategy. You need to do what's best for the company and cut ties with Joe before he sinks your entire team.

There have been times when I let my company suffer by keeping Joe around for too long. Looking back, I realize that my failure to fire Joe as soon as I knew he was a problem arose primarily out of fear. What will happen if I cut ties with Joe? What accounts are loyal to Joe and not necessarily to the company? Will Joe bolt for a competitor or compete directly against us? Even though I can't trust Joe, can I really afford to shake things up this early in the life of my company? These are legitimate fears, but remember, fear should never be the primary motivator driving your decisions. The most important thing is protecting your company and your purpose by dealing directly and swiftly with personalities that drag you and your team down.

The best route is to simply avoid hiring Joe at all. That way you don't have to deal with a toxic personality or navigate the uncomfortable prospects of firing somebody. Of course, you won't always hire the perfect people, and you'll most likely have to deal with difficult employees at one time or another, but knowing what to look for in a potential hire is a powerful tool to help you build the best team possible.

In his excellent book Good to Great, Jim Collins talks about putting the right people in the right seat on the bus.[27] It's a great analogy to keep in mind when you're building a team. Unfortunately, you usually don't have the chance to see exactly how a person will perform before hiring them. That's why you need to look for certain intangible qualities and traits that can give you a sense of what a person is like and how they're likely to influence your team. As you begin interacting with possible employees, use your gut to gauge the following intangibles:

1. **Do they put people first and focus on relationships in a positive way?** Even when you're hiring somebody whose primary responsibilities aren't interaction-oriented—like a number cruncher—this is always an important variable.

2. **Are they willing to take calculated risks as part of a larger team?** Determine if they are a "me" person or a "we" person. Are they willing to see the big picture and focus on the company's purpose over short-term personal needs?

3. **Will they buy into your purpose and company culture?** When interacting with a possible hire, detail to them as best you can

your company culture. See how excited (or not) they are about working in such an environment. Ginger and I spent many years carefully building our company culture, but there were always a few employees who were "above" it. They acted enthusiastic when it was discussed in group settings, but they ignored it the rest of the time. Our company would have been much more successful had we avoided those who didn't genuinely buy into our culture. If a person doesn't fit the fabric of your company's culture, or your company's culture doesn't fit the fabric of who they really are, then it's not a good fit and they should not be part of your team.

4. **Are they primarily motivated by personal achievement?** The best team players strike a balance between confidence and humility, self and team. Look for those who can show a good level of humility and who demonstrate a commitment to the team over more self-centered concerns.

5. **What drives them? As you interview and get to know possible team members,** try to figure out what gets them out of bed in the morning. In particular, look for people who love being part of something bigger than themselves and who will be motivated to work for the larger group purpose.

6. **Do they demonstrate congruency?** This is a hard one to determine at the outset, but you will get a good sense pretty quickly if a job candidate is the same person with you, the team, and the clients. If there are significant gaps between the person they are in each of these different settings, it will cause problems. If possible, try giving a job candidate a probationary employment period. During that time, pay attention to how they act in different situations and when they're around different people. Ideally, you're looking for people who have enough integrity to be the same person regardless of who they're with or what's going on around them.

As an example of red flags to watch out for, I once had an employee who would agree with team decisions in group meetings and express total buy-in, only to take a totally different stance when the group meeting was over, and he was in smaller groups or one-on-one with other employees. In every situation, he had to be the "good guy." There were even times when he would talk to me about why he thought another employee needed to be fired, and then afterward, would saddle up to that very person acting like he had nothing to do with the decision.

Always watch out for people who show signs of incongruence and who become completely different people based on who they're with and what they're doing. Avoid bringing people like this into your team. For more insights on the subject of congruency, check out Chapter 6 of *Launching Leaders: An Empowering Journey for a New Generation*.

Protect the Mothership

During the early months of your new business, as you are trying to attract and keep key team members, you may face situations in which you need to arrange "employment packages" for certain employees or new hires. If you don't do it right, this can put a lot of strain on the financial well-being of the company. These rules will help you focus on protecting the mothership:

1. **Before you consider giving any big rewards...**

   Make sure your startup has a verifiable track record of established sales and net income for at least several months running. There is a tendency during the first years of a new company to reward too handsomely before it's certain that the company's cash flow can actually sustain it. Whatever you do, never go into debt to attract and keep talent.

2. **Be prepared to sacrifice.**

   So far, this chapter has focused primarily on being careful with how much you give your team members, but the same applies to you as the business owner. In Chapter 3, I talked about the importance of saving up a cash reserve to assure a successful launch. This principle applies after launch, too. It takes time before a startup generates enough cash flow to allow distributions, including paying yourself a salary. In the early months, and possibly even years, keep the profits in the bank and build up a safety reserve to give your company a solid financial footing. Taking too much out of a young company too soon is a recipe for failure and is a big part of why only 10% of all startups make it past five years.

3. **Empower your soldiers who sacrifice for the good of the team.**

   As you evaluate the intangibles of each team member, look for those who will prioritize the health of the company over their own personal needs or desires. The best team members are the ones who understand that when the company is healthy, each individual's needs and aspirations are more likely to be met. Fill your team with soldiers who will strive for the success of the entire company, and who care about the larger purpose as much as you do.

Humility: The Secret Sauce for Building a Powerhouse Team

A large measure of your success will be determined by the quality of the team you assemble. But hiring the right people is only half the story. As team leader, you also need to orchestrate the growth of each individual employee as they strive to fill their roles within your company. A cohesive, powerful team will emerge as each individual works hard, grows, and improves.

As team leader, you need to develop skills and qualities that will earn the respect of your employees. Humility is quite possibly the single most important attribute for team leaders to have. Developing the right combination of humility and quiet confidence is how you lead your team with vision and power. Fortunately, humility can be learned and practiced. Here are a few ways to cultivate humility:

- **Turn outward and celebrate others.** Allow the light to shine on others and don't be a glutton for attention.

- **Actively seek feedback and implement it.** Even if the truth is hard to hear, be vulnerable.

- **Honor people who influence you.** Don't forget your mentors.

- **Empower others to do what you do.** Give freely of the gifts you possess, recognizing that you've gotten where you are thanks to the help of mentors, teachers, team members, and others who were willing to share with you.

- **Don't hoard knowledge.** The new generations demand to know the "why" behind the "what." Sharing information freely is crucial for building a strong team. Being willing to share your knowledge is also a trait of humility.

- **Listen.** A wise man once said . . . nothing.

- **Confront challenges with compassion and empathy.** Before jumping to conclusions or hasty judgments, put yourself in others' shoes. This is a powerful leadership trait that is fueled by humility.

- **Laugh at yourself.** Don't take yourself too seriously.

- **Say "thank you."** When people know you appreciate them, it makes all the difference.

Game On!

One of the Launching Leaders founders, Terry Pitts, is famous for the phrase "game on." He has been an inspiration to the Launching Leaders program, and whenever we're about to open classes in another country, expand to a new venue, or add something to our curriculum, he leads the charge by enthusiastically saying, "game on!"

I hope that you can enter the entrepreneurial game with this same attitude of optimism and excitement. Remember that to succeed in this game, you can't do it alone; you need a strong team working alongside you. Implementing the principles in this chapter will help you build the perfect team so you can grow a successful company, achieve your purpose, and make a positive impact on the world.

You don't want to just play the game. You want to win. Game on!

Chapter Summary

- Nobody succeeds alone. As an entrepreneur, your ability to succeed depends largely on the quality of the team you build.

- In your efforts to attract and keep the best talent, don't give away so much—whether money or stock—that you end up crippling the business or losing control of your company.

- Protect the mothership. If the company doesn't thrive, nobody wins, and your purpose will die.

- Exercise humility, the secret sauce for effective communication and leadership.

- Build your team and play to win. Game on!

Culture: Create an Atmosphere That Empowers

"The real competitive advantage in any business is one word only, which is 'people.'"

—Kamil Toume[28]

What do people mean when they say an organization has a good "culture?" Does it mean that everyone working there is having a great time? Does it mean every Friday is jeans day and there's ice cream in the lunch room? When someone says they hate the culture of the company they work for, what exactly are they referring to: their boss, their peers, some other element of their job?

To understand the concept of company culture, it's helpful to think about how a healthy family operates. No family, and no individual within a family, is perfect, yet every member of a functional family figures out how to work together for the good of the whole. As with our real-world families, nobody should expect a perfect or entirely drama-free work environment. But if a company has a strong and positive culture, then people will work through their differences to build relationships of trust and empowerment, and to achieve a shared purpose. Culture is what will get everyone in the same boat, rowing in the same direction—and when this happens, your company has a real shot at going somewhere spectacular.

In my experience, it takes several years of trial and error to create a meaningful company culture. With focused effort, Ginger and I successfully cultivated a culture at our company that reflected our core values and our larger purpose. In particular, we focused on creating a family-like atmosphere in which people felt safe, empowered, and comfortable working together. As a result, I believe most folks loved working at our organization. In fact, our employees often commented on how much they enjoyed working at a company where it felt more like a family rather than a cold corporation.

Culture defines companies in a fundamental way, setting the tone both for where a company goes and how it gets there. If a company is the incubator in which great ideas are born, then culture is the environment inside the incubator—it must be just right if you want great ideas to mature and come to life. Ultimately, culture will make or break your company, so never delegate to anybody else the task of creating the culture that will define your company. Culture must be highly individualized to each unique company, and it emanates from the heart and purpose of the entrepreneur.

Rather than try to give you a cookie-cutter, step-by-step approach for building culture, this chapter will outline the most important principles that will help you establish a culture that's right for you, your goals, your purpose, and your company.

The Importance of Culture

I first learned the importance of culture decades ago, years before Ginger and I started our own company. At the time, I was working for another firm as a regional sales rep and was in charge of selling and providing services to somewhere around 30 clients.

My single biggest revenue-producing client was also incredibly needy and difficult to work with. One Saturday, this client asked me to help him with something related to my company's products. I politely told him I had other pressing plans and would not be able to accommodate his request. He then called my boss, and before I knew it, my boss was calling me on the phone, demanding that I give up my Saturday to do whatever the client wanted, regardless of my previous plans. I pushed back, and my boss replied, "How much do you like your job?"

The reason I couldn't work that Saturday was because Ginger and our pre-maturely-born first child were in the hospital, our little son fighting for his life. Even though my boss knew this, he still threatened me and my family by putting my job on the line. I felt that this was a heartless demand, and it frightened me that he would force me to choose between my family and my job—especially during such a critical time. I chose my family.

This experience demolished all respect I had for my boss and for the company and gave me reason to step back and think about what had happened. I wondered how much better everything would have been if my boss had shown respect, compassion, and understanding with my family's situation. What if my boss would have said, "I understand our client wants your time in the morning, but knowing your situation, I'll be happy to fill in for you?" It would have been a vastly different experience and I would have gained more respect for my boss, rather than completely losing all trust in him.

This experience proved to be formative. Most immediately, it deepened my desire to break from this company and begin my path toward entrepreneurship. Beyond that, it also showed me how important it is to cultivate the right culture—a culture in which all team members feel respected, trusted, cared for, and understood. I reflected on this experience years later when Ginger and I were running our own company. As we thought about the environment we wanted to create, we focused on developing a culture that would lift everyone on our team to new heights.

Here are four principles that will guide your efforts to establish a culture of empowerment.

Principle 1: Be a "Level 5 Leader"

When Ginger and I decided to sell our company, one of our top priorities was finding a buyer who shared similar values and who would be committed to keeping alive the culture we had built. We were thrilled when we found someone who seemed like a perfect fit. Unfortunately, things didn't play out the way we thought they would and as often happens in an acquisition, there was a clash between the company culture Ginger and I had built and the culture of the purchasing company.

After the acquisition, I remained on board as an executive, but I became restless and uneasy as I watched the culture of our purchasers eat into the culture we had developed. I eventually confronted them about the ongoing culture clash to see if we could find any sort of compromise. These conversations ultimately fell apart and a few years later, I was forced out of the company.

This experience once again illustrated to me the power of culture. I was surprised that amidst the huge changes and tumult of the acquisition and subsequent merger, the factor that became by far the most important, urgent, and tense was culture.

Furthermore, my interactions with the executive team of the purchasing firm demonstrated that culture rolls down from the top. After having numerous conversations with them, I was struck by how thoroughly the executives embodied the values and attitudes reflected in their company's broader culture. It became abundantly clear that the way a leader conducts herself or himself really does set the tone for the rest of the company, not because employees mindlessly mimic their leaders, but because the attitudes at the top eventually permeate the entire organization.

That's why it's so important to be what Jim Collins calls a "level 5 leader." In his book Good to Great, Collins explains, "a level 5 leader is an individual who blends extreme personal humility with intense professional will. They channel their ego needs away from themselves and into the larger goal of building a great company. It's not that level 5 leaders have no ego or self-interest. Indeed, they are incredibly ambitious—but their ambition is first and foremost for the institution, not themselves."[29]

Since culture moves from the top down, you need to develop a culture that you genuinely believe in and that you are willing to live. In particular, focus on creating an environment that will empower all members of your team. To give you a more concrete sense of what it means to be a leader capable of building this type of culture, here are the key character traits of a level 5 leader:

1. *Level 5 leaders are a paradox* — On the one hand, they are highly ambitious, but their ambition is for the entire organization to excel. Level 5 leaders never let their ego get in the way because they are modest about what they personally contribute. They tend to be modest, understated, and self-effacing.

2. *Level 5 leaders are driven* — They feel an intense need to produce exceptional results on a sustainable basis, rather than grand one-off business maneuvers.

3. *Level 5 leaders build successors* — Great leaders know that their legacy will live on only if they give the next generation of leaders the mentorship they need to achieve even greater success.

4. *Level 5 leaders share the praise in good times and take the blame in bad times* — This is a powerful way to demonstrate humility, your commitment to being a team player, and to create a strong sense of loyalty and commitment among your employees.

5. *Level 5 leaders are never larger-than-life business celebrities* — Great leaders understand that creating a grandiose, awe-inspiring persona will smother the efforts of the rest of their team and they avoid this kind of grandstanding.

6. *Level 5 leaders come from within the organization* — The commitment to build an enduringly great company requires resolute diligence and hard work rather than grand, impressive, or overly-complex business moves.

At the end of the day, you simply cannot delegate the job of creating your company's culture. It comes from the top down. So be a level 5 leader and lead by example.

Principle 2: Build Around Your Purpose

I've already talked multiple times about the importance of defining your purpose before launching your new company. This is the foundation that will drive everything you and your employees do. Your purpose should also be the foundation of your company's culture.

I suggest coming up with a mantra that will reflect your purpose and help give concrete shape to the culture you're trying to establish.

A mantra is a single statement, or even just a few words, that frame your purpose and intent. For example, one of my companies adopted the mantra, "More than you expected," as a way of centering our overall purpose of delivering top-notch service to our clients. Some well-known company mantras you may have heard before include, "Rewarding everyday moments" (Starbucks) or, "When you care enough, you can change the world" (Hallmark). You can see how these mantras in some way reflect larger values and purposes and help set the tone for the general culture of each company.

After crafting a mantra that reflects your purpose and defines your culture, don't abandon it. Stick to it and put it into practice. In one of my previous companies, we had an unexpected chance to expand into a line of business that was totally outside our core business. But because one of our executives was experienced in this field, we decided to give it a shot. After a couple years of trying to make it work, this new venture was costing us over a million dollars annually, which forced us to lay off some very good employees.

This was frustrating for everyone. Looking back, the whole thing could easily have been avoided had we stuck with our mantra and some of our primary purposes, namely, be the best in our field and earn a sufficient level of profits from each client. Clearly, branching out into a field beyond our expertise was the exact opposite of these purposes. If we would have considered more carefully how that particular opportunity fit into our purpose—or in this case, how it didn't fit our purpose—we could have avoided trying to diversify in this counterproductive way. Sometimes it can be challenging to stay within the purpose, mantra, and culture you develop, but having the discipline to do so will pay big dividends and save you a lot of grief.

Principle 3: Start Simple and Keep It Simple

In the tech world there is a phenomenon called "feature creep." This is when developers try to add so many new features to a piece of software that it fails to ever achieve its original intent and it never goes anywhere.

When building culture, avoid feature creep. Keep your purpose, mantra, and culture clear and simple. Don't try to add so many endless little details that your culture becomes meaningless or so complicated that nobody can actually practice it. To be sure, your culture should always be dynamic, and you should always be open to adjusting it and letting it evolve over time, but never depart from your core purpose.

Back when I was founding my first company it was very popular for executives and boards of directors to go on "retreats," where we basically hibernated in a mountain cabin trying to develop a super complex "mission statement." We came up with an entire poster board of "stuff," had it professionally printed, hung it in our lobby, and never referenced it again. Why did our so-called mission statement hang there uselessly collecting dust? Because it was way too detailed and convoluted.

Remember, I like to paint with broad brush strokes, and this applies to creating a company culture as well.

Use your purpose to create a simple mantra, weave it into your culture and brand, and make it something simple, easy to understand, and actionable.

Principle 4: Give Back—Create a Common Cause

The final principle for establishing an empowering culture builds on the idea that your business efforts should do something greater than just make money. Every culture must include giving back charitably. It breathes a uniquely empowering sense of life, meaning, and purpose into the entire organization.

What I'm talking about here is creating a program that is part of the regular operations of your business and that is devoted entirely to giving back to good causes. To be effective, this plan must include everyone on your team and it must be tailored to your unique organization.

As an example, when Ginger and I first learned this principle, we decided to set aside a certain percentage of our company's revenue and donate it to the charity of our client's choice. We engaged a firm to vet their choices to make sure there wasn't any monkey business, and then every year, we tallied up the total revenue we made from each client and gave a percentage of it away to whichever charity that client chose. All in all, our company gave to nearly 100 charities.

This was powerful because it showed our clients and our employees that we were more than just a money-hungry company. We were an organization that cared about our community and that was committed to making a positive impact. We quickly added an extra component in which Ginger and I, along with our employees, also volunteered our time at certain charities, thereby making the entire experience more personal and interconnected.

When Ginger and I first implemented our giving back program, we didn't know how we were going to afford it, since it was based on gross revenue, not profits. But amazingly, we had our best years in both revenue and profit after we launched the program. I think part of the reason for that was that our clients understood that the more business they did with us, the more their favorite charities would benefit. On top of that, I also believe that our giving back program resonated deeply with our employees, motivating them and confirming that our company was more than just a place to work; it was a team passionately devoted to worthy causes.

The bottom line is that everyone wants to feel like they're a part of something bigger than themselves. As soon as we instituted a giving back program into our business plan, all of us—Ginger and I, our employees, and our clients—felt a deeper sense of connection and purpose.

After seeing just how empowering this experience was for everyone involved, I am a firm believer that every single organization must include a program for giving back. This is crucial for cultivating a culture of empowerment. An active giving back program will help you attract and keep talented employees who have a genuine interest in being part of your team and who want more out of a job than simply making money.

Additional Resources

As you work to develop your company's culture, take a look at the following books:

- *The Five Dysfunctions of a Team* by Patrick Lencioni
- *Good to Great* by Jim Collins
- *The Art of the Start* by Guy Kawasaki
- *Launching Leaders: An Empowering Journey for a New Generation* by Steven A. Hitz

Cultivating a healthy and productive culture is a vital element of entrepreneurial success. As you work hard to grow your business, be sure that you put in the effort to carefully establish a culture aimed at empowering your team, associates, and clients, and that will help you achieve your ultimate purpose.

Chapter Summary

- Every company will in one way or another develop a culture, so be sure that you consciously and carefully cultivate a culture that is in line with your values, goals, and purpose.

- Culture comes from the top—do not delegate the task of creating culture.

- Remember the four principles that will help you create a culture that is both empowering and tailored to your unique company:

    1. Be a level 5 leader and lead by example.

    2. Build around your purpose. Craft a brief and memorable mantra that reflects your purpose and gives concrete shape to the culture you're trying to build.

    3. Avoid "feature creep" and keep your purpose, mantra, and culture simple, easy to understand, and actionable.

    4. Make giving back a key aspect of your company's culture and identity.

The Power of Leverage

___

"Attempting to succeed without embracing the tools immediately available for your success is no less absurd than trying to row a boat by drawing only your hands through the water or trying to unscrew a screw using nothing more than your fingernails."

—Richie Norton[30]

One of the most ingenious components on an airplane is the trim tab, a tiny, adjustable surface located on the trailing edge of a larger control surface, such as a rudder or wing. The purpose of a trim tab is to stabilize the airplane and keep it moving on its intended course. There are usually two sets of trim tabs on an airplane, 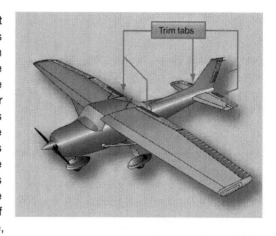 one for the horizontal axis of flight and the other for the vertical axis.

Having flown my own aircraft for many years, I know the incredible impact those tiny trim tabs make. When adjusted properly, they allow the pilot to fly virtually hands-free, without needing to apply pressure to the yoke or controls. This gives the pilot freedom to pay attention to other pressing matters in the cockpit.

Trim tabs are the perfect analogy for introducing the concept of leverage, which, just like trim tabs, is all about using relatively small resources to gain a much larger advantage. When you learn to effectively leverage your strengths as an entrepreneur, you gain much-needed control, clout, or pull so that you can keep your company flying smoothly on its intended course. Leverage, like trim tabs, lets you maximize your time and effort. It enables you to take your hands off the controls and focus on other important tasks without worrying that your company will drift off track.

Effectively leveraging your resources lets you maximize your results far beyond what would be possible on your own. A great example of this is buying a home. When you take out a mortgage, you leverage whatever cash you have to gain access to a much larger amount of money, making it possible to buy a home worth 5 to 10 times more than what you could afford by yourself.

When it comes to entrepreneurism, you can leverage all sorts of resources: money, intelligence, time, relationships, and more. This chapter will teach you how to effectively leverage your strengths and assets so you can chart a direct course to success.

Leveraging Time

The concept of leveraging time is interesting because each of us has the exact same amount of it every single day: 24 hours. Yet, some people seem to get much more done with their time than others. These are the people who know how to leverage time to their benefit. They know how to get the most out of the precious time they're given each day.

Leveraging time is tricky—that's why there are entire industries devoted to teaching people how to use time effectively and to creating time management products. The most powerful time management tool I've ever found doesn't have anything to do with these commercially-marketed methods. It's a basic, step-by-step system for daily living that was developed by my mentor over the course of his career. He calls it simply The Formula.[31]

While I'm not going to outline each step of The Formula in this book, I will focus on the one step that directly has to do with time: Get Up Early. This may sound simple, and it is. That's the beauty of it. When you have the discipline to get up early, you instantly give yourself access to more time each day, which means you have the chance to pursue activities that you might not otherwise be able to. In particular, I suggest you use the additional time you create each morning to practice Daily Mindfulness, ponder your purpose, journal, or any of the other pursuits outlined in Chapter 3. You will be amazed by how much more you accomplish when you make yourself wake up and get the day started a little bit earlier.

Leveraging Relationships—Use or Abuse?

According to the cliché, it's not what you know, but who you know that counts. I say it's both what you know and who you know. This is important for entrepreneurs to understand because there will be numerous times when you and your team will ask yourselves, "Who do we know that can help us with this issue?" Or, "Who can connect us with someone who can help?" In these moments, you will need to leverage your relationships.

Obviously, since we're talking about how you interact with other people, this needs to be treated with great care. Leveraging relationships will only work if you offer the same level of support and collaborative spirit that you look for in your moments of need.

Broadly speaking, there are two types of people: those who drag others down and those who help others move forward. You probably already know people who fit into each category. On the one hand, there's that person who shows up only when they need something from you. They never give anything back or offer any help, they only take from the relationship. I call this type of person an "abuser." These are the people who drag you down.

On the other hand, there are those friends who show up without any sort of agenda and who genuinely care about you. They're as interested in giving as they are in receiving. These people create symbiotic flows that benefit everyone involved. These are the relationships you can leverage in a positive way.

To illustrate what I'm talking about, let me share personal examples of each type of person. I once had a friend ask if he could visit me at my home to discuss something "exciting" with me. I agreed and was very disappointed when he showed up to pitch me on a multi-level marketing scheme. It turns out this person was simply trying to pull me into his "down line" in order to benefit himself financially. I was annoyed that my friend apparently thought so little of me that he hadn't been upfront with me about the purpose of his visit, and that he surprised me with what felt like a manipulative ambush. The whole experience was negative and taught me to beware friends who are really wolves in sheep's clothing.

In stark contrast to this experience, I had another friend who showed up at my house within hours of learning that I'd been terminated by the people who bought my company. Knowing how much I struggle with technology, this person came over to help set up my computer system. I'd previously relied on using the equipment and software provided by my former job and after being terminated, I suddenly found myself stuck without basic technology.

This friend did everything for free—in fact, they made it clear that I would not be allowed to pay for their services. This isn't necessarily an example of leveraging relationships, but it's an excellent example of what a healthy, positive, and mutually beneficial relationship looks like. I had helped this person many times in the past and they were happy to lend me a hand when I needed it.

The key to all this is to realize that the best relationships are two-way streets. Seek ways to give rather than take, and you will be able to leverage your connections with others in a way that is authentic, natural, and that moves both of you forward.

Leveraging Credit and Credibility

A few years ago, my family hired a wonderful farmer to take care of our farm. One day, while talking to him about finding new places for our cows to graze, I asked him about the acreage across the road. He quickly identified the land owner by name and said, "You don't want to do any business with that guy. He owes me money and he owes my dad money too." End of discussion and end of consideration.

You can always leverage a good reputation, but if you've tarnished your reputation the way our neighbor had, you lose your credibility. Had this land owner been trustworthy, he would have maintained a good reputation and we could have built a new connection that might have blessed each of our lives.

I began recognizing the power of credibility early in my career. At one point, when my first company was still in its infancy, I found myself very tight on cash when payroll was due. I had no way to pay my workers that week—a truly gut-wrenching experience for a new entrepreneur.

Fortunately, I'd built a strong relationship with my banker, who knew me as a friend and not just a business. I had built a strong reputation with him because he knew that in prior years I had chosen to pay off a large debt instead of filing for bankruptcy. As a result, he knew I would never do anything to harm others and this gave me a lot of credibility in his eyes. I told him about my payroll predicament and without question, he went above and beyond his basic duties to arrange a line of credit for me. I was able to pay my employees, and a short time later, I paid off the credit he extended me. I have never forgotten that favor. In time, we became one of his largest-deposit clients, and he and I invested in many ventures together over the years.

The moral of the story: Keep your credit high and your credibility even higher.

Leveraging Debt

Whether you're a startup company or a 100-year-old corporation, debt is a standard part of the financial equation. When you borrow money intelligently and strategically, you can leverage your debt to pull off some heavy lifting and to accomplish more than you could on your own.

There are three main keys to ensure that your debt is empowering rather than damaging:

1. Be sure that your cash flow and revenue capabilities are substantial enough to pay back your debt in a timely manner without crippling your company.

2. Whatever debt you take must directly advance your company's opportunities.

3. The interest rates at which you borrow should be low enough that the money you borrow allows you to make more money in a shorter amount of time than if you hadn't taken the loan.

When my family and I first started our farm, we needed new sprinkler irrigation pivots. When we purchased the farm, the equipment was in such poor shape we couldn't attract anybody to help us manage it. New sprinkler pivots were not a choice, they were a requirement.

Recognizing the importance of making this purchase immediately, we borrowed money, bought the pivots, and went to work. Thanks to the new equipment, the farm had the most productive harvest in its entire history. We were able to depreciate half the cost of the pivots in the first year and we put ourselves on pace to pay back the entire loan within three years, all while continually improving crop production and growing revenues.

This is an excellent example of wise debt, as it gave us the cash we needed to make a purchase that we couldn't otherwise afford and that immediately improved our business. We leveraged that debt for the good of the entire company.

On the other hand, unwise debt would be something like buying company cars for high-ranking employees. This kind of debt doesn't produce anything concrete for the company other than making a couple people happy about receiving a cool perk. This is not how you leverage debt effectively; this is not wise debt.

Other Ways to Leverage Your Strengths

This chapter has covered the four most vital resources that you must learn to leverage effectively: time, relationships, credit and credibility, and debt. I also invite you to explore additional ways to increase your advantage by leveraging other strengths, assets, and opportunities. These questions will point you in the right direction:

How can I leverage professional achievements and moments of success?

If you receive an award or public recognition, how can you leverage that toward even greater success? Such events are great opportunities to build up some excitement around your brand. You can use press releases, marketing or advertising campaigns, and especially social media to make modest announcements and to spread the word.

How can I leverage my education and my attempts to be a lifelong learner?

If you'll remember from Chapter 3, one of the best ways to invest in yourself is to become a lifelong learner. There are numerous ways you can leverage all that learning for the benefit of your business.

One idea that I'm a big fan of is looking for moments to share little tidbits of knowledge with colleagues, employees, or clients. In particular, focus on communicating information that's relevant and current, as this will be the most beneficial to the people you're interacting with and will demonstrate how up to date you are in your field.

Who doesn't want to work with somebody who has a constant reservoir of relevant knowledge and productive insight? Learning to communicate things you learn can build trust and confidence between you and the people you work with. Just be sure you communicate effectively. Don't preach at others or try to elevate yourself above others, and don't talk in a way that makes you look like a know-it-all. To avoid coming across the wrong way, always communicate from a place of authenticity, passion, and a genuine commitment to the collaborative success.

How can I leverage my talents and skills?

You have gifts and talents that you've developed throughout your life. Put them to good use by looking for ways to freely share your gifts and talents with those around you, especially if you can help somebody in a moment of need. This will demonstrate your depth of character and is one of the most powerful ways to build strong connections of trust and respect. Many times, this kind of service pays off down the road when you find yourself in a scenario where you need to leverage a positive relationship.

How can I leverage my team's unique skills and talents?

Recognize that everyone has something to offer. Focus on hiring team members whose unique skill sets complement yours and that help build a well-rounded, capable organization. Every successful company has experts on the team, folks who are working hard to apply The 10,000 Hour Rule and whose expertise can differentiate their organization from all others. These are the people you want. Seek out those whose skills are marketable, relevant, and who can help your company move closer to achieving your primary purpose.

How can I leverage my communication skills?

Have you ever noticed that people who can communicate effectively—especially those who can tell powerful and engaging stories—seem more likely to excel?

Effective storytelling is the key to great communication. Stories are a powerful way to communicate because they activate and engage multiple parts of the brain simultaneously: language processing, information processing, emotions, and even our more reflexive flight-or-fight responses.

Fortunately, this is a skill that can be learned. When you develop your communication and storytelling skills, you can leverage them in some pretty powerful ways. Believe me, it is well worth your time to learn this art. For a detailed discussion of communication and storytelling, see Chapter 10 of *Launching Leaders: An Empowering Journey for a New Generation*.

Chapter Summary

- Leveraging your various resources, assets, and opportunities is how you build "trim tabs" to keep your organization flying toward your purpose.

- Leveraging your resources empowers you to achieve more with less.

- Learn how to effectively leverage:

  - Time

  - Relationships

  - Credit and Credibility

  - Debt

- Begin looking for additional resources to leverage for the benefit of your company, including achievements, awards, knowledge, communication skills, and more.

Don't Be Poisoned
By Success

———

"Character cannot be developed in ease and quiet. Only through experience of trial and suffering can the soul be strengthened, vision cleared, ambition inspired, and success achieved."

– Helen Keller[32]

The life of an entrepreneur moves at warp speed. Before you even realize it, you are suddenly celebrating your twentieth year in business or preparing to sell your company. For years, you lived on the edge, scraping, sacrificing, and giving so much of yourself to your company that you probably missed out on some important aspects of your everyday life. You gave up family outings, had to miss some of your kid's sports games, maybe even forgot your partner's birthday or your anniversary at some point.

During your startup years, you took big risks and worked as hard as you possibly could to sustain a competitive advantage and secure a predictable cash flow, all with the hopes of someday turning a profit. You were anxious for your "A" team to eventually come together, all singing from the same hymn book and enjoying the culture you worked hard to foster. You knew that most startups fold at the dreaded one-year and five-year marks, yet you risked it all and took the leap anyway, pressing on toward your purpose and figuring out what your company needed to do to survive.

Somewhere along the way, you discovered that leading a company wasn't so much about profits, but people. Your primary purpose—the purpose driving your life and your entrepreneurial activities—became the centerpiece. You learned how to use your business efforts to give back and make a positive impact on the world. You learned that finances are only one part of what it means to be a successful entrepreneur. Finally, after sacrificing so much, working so hard, giving it your all—and hopefully having fun along the way!—the rocket you spent so many years wheeling to the launch pad successfully blasted off into space. You paid the price for your success, and you're hoping it was all worth it.

The scenario I just outlined is relatively unique, as most entrepreneurs never make it that far. And for the few entrepreneurs who do make it, entirely new challenges suddenly crop up—many of which arise out of success itself.

In many ways, success has its own dark side that you must be prepared to deal with if you want to be an entrepreneur. With sizable profits comes comfort, company bloat, heightened competition, and a new set of financial demands and constraints, including more employees and HR departments that constantly press for higher salaries.

Similarly, because a successful company will almost always become significantly larger than it was during its startup phase, you have to deal with communication challenges across large office spaces, geographical distance, and different time zones. Some of your team members may misunderstand your purpose, or have purposes of their own, and they may start building their own private silos and creating their own loyalties with other workers in order to pull in directions different from the one you've established.

As your company grows, you will need to create new departments and the organizational chart gets increasingly complex. The board retreat becomes more focused on finding the most luxurious hotel rather than diving into a serious discussion of strategy. Your management team gradually morphs into a group of well-groomed caretakers, and the simplicity of what you started out doing starts feeling like a labyrinth with no easy way out.

Depressed yet? Even though it sounds bad, don't be too upset. While it's important to understand that these challenges will arise, you should also know that there are ways to avoid letting them poison you, your company, or your success. Here are 5 "antidotes" to the poisons that arise when you begin achieving success.

Antidote 1: Don't Trade Leadership for Popularity

When I was a lay minister for a young adult congregation, a big part of my role was counseling, encouraging, and generally helping the members of my congregation chart their course through life. Some of them faced Mount Everest-sized challenges, and I became the Sherpa guiding them over the rough terrain.

During the process of advising and counseling, I found that I wanted to please everyone. I wanted to be the hero responsible for getting them all to the summit. It bothered me that in some cases this simply was not possible. Not everyone would succeed on their first, second, or third attempts—some might never make it all the way to summit. Some parishioners needed to go back to base camp and try for the summit another time. Sometimes, people needed to retreat first before they had the strength to advance.

I was so caught up in my sincere desire to help guide them all to the top that I failed to recognize that often, mini-defeats are actually the early steps of progress. When people didn't immediately improve or advance toward their goals the way I hoped they would, I was bothered because I couldn't live up to my self-imposed role of super hero.

I eventually went to my ecclesiastical leader for advice. He told me, "Your ministry is not a popularity contest. The direction and counsel you give will not always be popular. There will be those who don't find success and peace on your watch."

This was a hard lesson for me to learn, but it was an important one. It's also a lesson that translates well into the business world. The best leaders are not necessarily the most popular ones. In fact, if you try too hard to be popular with everyone, or to be each and every person's hero, you're setting yourself up for failure.

Instead, lead with conviction and stay focused on your purpose and values. Live and teach sound principles that will lead to the realization of your most important goals. You don't need to assure individual success for each person on your team to be a great leader and you don't need to be popular to gain respect. You don't have to please everyone. Focus on achieving your purpose with integrity and everything else will fall into place.

Antidote 2: Don't Let Your Generosity Create Entitlement

When my company had grown and become profitable, I faced an unexpected dilemma. For some reason, I felt that I would lose respect or that I was committing some sort of immoral act if I didn't pay myself and every team member more or less equally.

I simply could not separate myself from the army of soldiers leading the charge on the ground. Perhaps part of these feelings arose from my unrealistic desire to be everyone's best friend. One way or another, these feelings and worries resulted in my giving away stock, country club memberships, very large financial rewards, and in the long run, none of it helped the company. In fact, it became an unintended problem, as some team members became more concerned with what they felt they were entitled to than with contributing to the larger team effort.

Before I go any further, let me be very clear. I am not arguing against taking care of your team. Being a good leader means caring for your people and paying them well. What I'm talking about is giving away rewards unnecessarily and frivolously, to the point that it becomes counterproductive and irresponsible. One of the biggest dangers of doing this is that you end up incentivizing a selfish sense of entitlement rather than a focus on pitching in to achieve the larger purpose. If you create entitlement, you also fertilize the ground for silos to grow, as people lose sight of the team picture and focus only on themselves.

The antidote to this is to keep an accurate perspective on the growth of your company, the roles played by different team members, and the goals you are still working to achieve. For starters, you need to recognize that there is nothing wrong with separating out your financial rewards from those of your employees. You were the primary risk taker from the very beginning, so you should feel justified in paying yourself more than a team member who was hired later on in the process. Again, I'm not saying give yourself so much that there's nothing left for anybody else. Rather, you need to strike a healthy balance between taking care of your team and rewarding yourself for the risk, sacrifice, dedication, and hard work you put into starting and growing your business.

Additionally, keep in mind that you still have other objectives to achieve. If you squander your company's resources by irresponsibly giving things away, you may jeopardize those goals. The greatest benefit of properly channeling your generosity is that it allows you to maintain the financial freedom to pursue your broader purposes and goals, such as giving back and serving others outside your company.

In the end, you need to treat your team well without becoming irresponsible in your generosity. As soon as I started giving things out frivolously, the dynamics among and between team members began changing. In some cases, it brought out the worst in people. Unfortunately, many people revealed themselves to be fake friends whose commitment to the team was measured only by the size of their paychecks and the perks they received.

Remember that you build loyalty and respect through practicing correct principles and values, not by creating unsustainable expectations. Keep your true friends close and your checkbook even closer and you will achieve the right balance for long-term success.

Antidote 3: Don't Delegate Beyond Your Ability to Stay Connected

As your company grows, it will become too large for you to be personally acquainted with every single aspect of what's going on. You will be required to delegate certain duties and responsibilities, but never delegate so much that you become disconnected from the day-to-day operations of your company. Effective delegation frees you up to focus on larger, more pressing concerns without becoming disconnected.

To accomplish this, I like the concept of "MBWA"—Management by Walking Around. MBWA is all about getting out of your office and making sure you're spending some of your time with the rank and file. Observe how they do their jobs, ride with them on assignments, watch, and listen.

When my company grew into a large entity, I didn't do a very good job of this. I delegated beyond my ability to stay connected, and unhealthy divisions between different members of the team began to crop up.

Learn from my mistakes and stay connected by following these five tips:

1. Hold monthly one-on-one interviews with each of your direct reports. Always review how their duties are aligned with the larger purpose and values of the company. Listen intently.

2. Know when your direct reports are holding meetings with their staff and drop in unannounced from time to time. You will immediately know whether or not they're pulling the wagon in the same direction as you. Don't sit in on these meetings to hear yourself talk; just observe and listen.

3. Take time to go back to the ground level. If you used to run the equipment during the initial startup days, then make sure you take time every once in a while to get back in the saddle. Stay connected to the passions, interests, and activities that initially sparked your desire to start the business in the first place. Get back in the trenches and enjoy it!

4. Spend enough time mingling around the water fountain or lunch room to know the hearts and minds of your rank and file employees. Remember, you don't have to be everyone's best friend, but you should spend enough time out of your office to have a general sense of how people are feeling about the company and what they're talking about.

5. As you implement each of these tips into your management style, always show genuine gratitude for every associate you interact with. Be a person of grace and understanding.

Southwest Airlines co-founder and former CEO Herb Kelleher is a great example of a business leader who knew how to stay connected with his employees. At one point, when he realized that the night shift employees were never able to attend company parties because of their work schedules, he showed up at an airport at two in the morning to host a BBQ for them.

By connecting with his workers, Kelleher built an unusually positive relationship between his management team and the leaders of the union to which most of his workers belonged. The union leader, Tom Burnett, described Kelleher by saying, "Lemme put it this way: how many CEOs do you know who come in to the cleaners' break room at 3 a.m. on a Sunday passing out doughnuts or putting on a pair of overalls to clean a plane?"[33] Clearly, Kelleher knew how to find the balance between delegating and staying connected.

Antidote 4: Don't Breathe Your Own Air

Achieving success can be a heady thing. The prestige can be intoxicating, and who doesn't want to be recognized as a winner? As you begin tasting success in your entrepreneurial life, remember the importance of being a level 5 leader (see Chapter 7), and when folks want to heap accolades on you, remind yourself of these key points:

- You are always one heartbeat away from death. This sounds melodramatic and ominous, but it's the truth. Strive to be the kind of person and leader that people will remember long after you have passed away. Lead so that whenever you leave this life, you will also leave behind a powerful legacy of positivity. And along the way, don't take yourself too seriously; the earth isn't going to implode when you leave.

- Don't become addicted to praise and public recognition, and don't become a person who always has to be the center of attention. I'm not saying you need to lurk in the shadows or downplay your expertise or success, but whatever you do, be humble, grateful, and always acknowledge that your success is shared by the entire team.

- When somebody tries to make a big deal about celebrating you, try to understand their intent. In many cases, people will try to leverage your success for their gain. Anytime somebody seeks to celebrate you, or give you some sort of award or honor, make sure their intent is to do something good and positive for the broader community and not just for somebody's individual benefit. Always be gracious, but also be careful if you sense that those heaping praise on you are in any way insincere.

Antidote 5: Success Doesn't Make You an Expert on Everything

I am still amazed when folks look to me for answers to their questions or concerns solely because I am a successful entrepreneur.

If the person's question is something I actually know something about, then I try to help as much as I can—sharing relevant expertise is part of giving back. But very often, people ask me about things outside my field, and when that happens, I've realized it is much more productive to simply acknowledge that I am as ignorant on that specific topic as the person asking the question.

Never make it look like you're an expert when you're not. This is pure posturing and self-aggrandizement. Instead, recognize that it makes you an even better expert to simply say, "You know, that is not in my wheelhouse, but I think I can connect you with someone who can help."

I often think of Auguste Rodin's famous sculpture "The Thinker," which shows a man deep in thought. It looks like he is pondering some very important things, and it gives the impression that this man will eventually wake from his meditation, raise his head, and speak only the most incredible pearls of wisdom. But he's naked. To me, this serves as a reminder that he is a human just like the rest of us. He has strengths and weaknesses; he is an expert in some things and ignorant about others.

As you become a successful entrepreneur, people will look up to you and they will turn to you for wisdom. When this happens, remember "The Thinker." Your success and expertise don't make you better than anyone else, and just like the person seeking your advice, you are knowledgeable about some things and ignorant of others. Be appreciative of the respect people show when they think you have the answer but be humble enough to acknowledge when you actually don't have a clue. Steering clear of the temptation to be everybody's expert will also help you avoid breathing your own egotistical air.

Final Thoughts

Whenever I think about my experiences mingling with highly successful people, I'm always struck by how amazing it is to meet an incredibly successful person who is down to earth, humble, and not at all self-absorbed. If you're like me, you love interacting with people like this, who understand that nobody succeeds alone and who maintain a clear sense of purpose in everything they do.

Like these folks, you have control over how you handle success. If your success is grounded in your core values and your purpose, then you will be equipped to handle success with grace, humility, and authenticity. Use the "antidotes" outlined in this chapter to fight off the poisons that success brings, and you will become that person who everyone loves to meet, and of whom people will say, "They sure were normal and humble for being such a big success."

Chapter Summary

- Success brings a new set of challenges, many of which stem from the fact that your homegrown business has exploded in size, scope, and value.

- Rely on these antidotes to avoid being poisoned by these new challenges:

    1. Don't trade leadership for popularity.

    2. Don't allow your generosity to create entitlement.

    3. Don't delegate beyond your ability to stay connected.

    4. Don't breathe your own air.

    5. Success doesn't make you an expert on everything.

Conclusion: Follow Your Passion

"The one thing that you have that nobody else has is you. Your voice, your mind, your story, your vision. So write and draw and build and play and dance and live as only you can."

—Neil Gaiman[34]

In *Grit: The Power of Passion and Perseverance*, Angela Duckworth shares some powerful insights that are relevant to everything I've written in this book. Discussing what it takes to become truly great, she writes:

"Who are the people at the very top of your field? What are they like? What do you think makes them special? . . . No matter the domain, the highly successful had a kind of ferocious determination that played out in two ways. First, these exemplars were unusually resilient and hardworking. Second, they knew in a very, very deep way what it was they wanted. They not only had determination, they had direction. It was this combination of passion and perseverance that made high achievers special. In a word, they had grit."[35]

I love how Duckworth explains that the secret to outstanding achievement is never talent alone. Instead, achievers have what she calls "grit"—a passion to excel coupled with the perseverance needed to complete difficult tasks. According to Duckworth, if you have the desire and perseverance to relentlessly pursue your passion, success will eventually follow.

Sometimes, your efforts to accomplish something meaningful may not be appreciated immediately—possibly not even in your lifetime. But if you continue following your passion anyway, the butterfly will eventually leave its cocoon and fly across the earth in vibrant color.

While I was in the middle of writing this book, my friend, Jim Parke, introduced me to a book titled *Endurance: Shackleton's Incredible Voyage* that perfectly illustrates what I'm talking about in this chapter.[36] The book, which recounts the experiences of Sir Ernest Shackleton's failed 1914 attempt to cross Antarctica, was written by Alfred Lansing and was originally published in 1959. Lansing's prose is powerful, simultaneously telling an incredible story and providing insights that taught me some important life lessons. *Endurance* is a truly one-of-a-kind book and I'm grateful that my friend introduced me to it.

The story of the book's creation, publication, and rise to fame is just as intriguing and powerful as the narrative it tells. Lansing studied journalism, and while he was working as a freelance writer he happened to learn about Sir Ernest Shackleton's experiences. Lansing became obsessed with the story, and in 1957, he decided to research it further. He contacted the few surviving members of the expedition, scoured the journals of shipmates, and pored over whatever materials he could find about Shackleton's doomed adventure. He then put his journalistic skills to work and in 1959, Endurance was published.

Initially, the book received good reviews but failed to achieve any sustained commercial success. Lansing died in 1975, at the age of 54, as an editor of a weekly newspaper in Connecticut. Endurance was still relatively obscure at the time of his passing.

Then, in 1986, a publisher for Carroll and Graf named Kent Carroll purchased the rights to Endurance. The company re-printed it and this time the book took off. It has since become a perennial best seller and is now in its forty-ninth printing. Commenting on the timing of the book's popularity, Lansing's wife, Barbara, said, "He would have been so proud, and yet he never knew."[37]

Lansing's experience, and the book's delayed path to success, drives home the point I want to leave you with. If you follow your passion with determination and integrity, implementing the principles you've learned in this book, you will leave an enduring legacy—even if you don't immediately see the results of your hard work.

Now that you've reached the end of this book, it is my hope that the principles you've learned will become the building blocks of your success. It will take hard work and discipline to implement these principles into your life and business, but if you do, you will be empowered to pursue your passion with vision and authenticity. Like Alfred Lansing, may you find the mentors that spark your passion, may you have the grit to endure, and may you make a positive impact on the lives of those around you. Onward!

Afterword

"You cannot get through a single day without having an impact on the world around you. What you do makes a difference, and you have to decide what kind of difference you want to make."

—Jane Goodall[88]

I've often heard people say they want to do something in their work that makes a difference or that has meaning beyond themselves. This most often is voiced by either young people with high ideals who are entering the workforce, or by disgruntled employees who find themselves in unfulfilling jobs.

The drive to do something meaningful is incredible and ennobling, and while many people have this dream, it is really only accomplished by a few. This book has given you and your generation a means by which you can accomplish this great goal.

There are so many people out there who are striving for success. But for many in the rising generations it isn't just about success, but what kind of success a person is trying to achieve. *Entrepreneurial Foundations for 20- and 30-Somethings* embraces these desires for meaningful and principled success and attempts to provide a conceptual framework that will empower you to make those desires real.

I have a good friend who works as an electrical engineer for a large reputable tech company. He designs microprocessor chips that run many of the world's mobile devices. Over the years his company has paid him well with both salary and stock options. He has been wise with his money, and while supporting a rather large family, has managed to save enough to pay off his house and afford other things like education for his children and a new car or two. His financial future looks bright.

But this friend, who sits in his cubicle designing microchips, frequently wonders if there is something more. He asks if his life as an individual contributor in a big company is really doing any good. He questions whether he's making a difference when he designs a speedier, more efficient computer chip that will soon become obsolete and replaced by the next chip he himself is tasked with creating. He wonders what might have happened if he had chosen a different path. As he wonders, he remembers his paid-off house, his children's education, and the new cars. Then he stops wondering... for a while.

Please understand, there is absolutely nothing wrong with being an electrical engineer who designs microchips. As Steve Hitz notes throughout this book, contributing to a corporate environment in a conscientious way is indeed important, both for the individual and the economy at large. But many in the rising generations are asking themselves if this is the path for them. They want to make a difference now, and many don't think they'll accomplish that if they're stuck working inside a cubicle. They want to get out on their own and change the world.

Could these notions be the naivety of youth or, as many would try to frame it, the unrealistic imagination of an entitled generation?

I don't think so. As far as I can tell, the rising generation isn't entitled; they have high expectations. Similarly, I don't see imagination as a baseless or overly idealistic fantasy, but as the first step toward building a new reality. In fact, one of the great things taught in this book—and in Launching Leaders more broadly—is the ability of young people (and forward-thinking older folks), to create the futures they imagine. So much of what can be accomplished in life is wrapped up in how you define yourself (your core values and your purpose), the plans you make for your life, and the mentors you surround yourself with. *Entrepreneurial Foundations* teaches you how to weave all this together, so you can make the jump into the exciting, stressful, demanding, thrilling, and ultimate world of creativity that is the entrepreneurial life.

After reading this book, seriously pondering in your gut what you most desire out of life, finding what drives you, and discovering what you are really meant to do, you're either ready to dive into the self-made world of entrepreneurship and make it happen, or it's time to climb into the cubicle to make your contribution that way.

I have lived in both worlds, and while I believe both are honorable, I also believe that entrepreneurism's inherent freedom will give you the best chance to create the vibrant future of your imagination. You decide.

Michael Leonard
Executive Director
Launching Leaders Worldwide Inc.
www.LLworldwide.org

Notes

[1] Brown, Antonio. *"Journey Quotes."* BrainyQuotes. https://www.brainyquote.com/topics/journey.

[2] Stein, Joel. *"The Greatest New Generation: Why Millennials Will Save Us All."* TIME May 20, 2013.

[3] Merriam-Webster, *"Livelihood,"* accessed February 13, 2018. https://www.merriam-webster.com/dictionary/ livelihood.

[4] See Chapter 2, *Launching Leaders: An Empowering Journey for a New Generation.*

[5] Quoted in *Change Your Future, Now! Questions, Reflections & Answers* by Germain Decelles (Québec, Canada: WebTech Management and Publishing Incorporated, 2013), 130.

[6] Adams, Susan. *"Most Americans Are Unhappy At Work."* Forbes June 20, 2014. https://www.forbes.com/sites/susanadams/2014/06/20/most-americans-are-unhappy-at-work/#5ab685d4341a.

[7] Quoted in *The Tao of Leadership: Lao Tzu's Tao Te Ching Adapted for a New Age* by John Heider (New York: Bantam, 1986), 22.

[8] Geraci, John. *"Embracing Bad Ideas To Get To Good Ideas."* Harvard Business Review December 27, 2016. https://hbr.org/2016/12/embracing-bad-ideas-to-get-to-good-ideas.

[9] Quoted in *"Work Smarter and More Easily by 'Sharpening Your Axe'"* by Melanie Pinola. Lifehacker June 21, 2011. https://lifehacker.com/5814019/work-smarter-and-more-easily-by-sharpening-your-axe.

[10] Quoted in *Introduction to Meditations: A New Translation by Marcus Aurelius,* Introduction by Gregory Hays (New York: The Modern Library, 2002), xxxvii.

[11] For a detailed, step-by-step guide for defining your purpose and establishing your core values, see Chapter 2 in *Launching Leaders: An Empowering Journey for a New Generation.*

[12] Gladwell, Malcolm. *Outliers: The Story of Success* (New York: Little, Brown and Company, 2008).

[13] Ibid., 39.

[14] Ibid., 40.

[15] For a detailed discussion of the importance of mentors, as well as a step-by-step guide for finding and adopting great mentors, see Chapter 3 of *Launching Leaders: An Empowering Journey for a New Generation.*

[16] For a detailed, step-by-step guide for creating your own financial plan similar to the one I described here, see Chapter 8 of *Launching Leaders: An Empowering Journey for a New Generation.*

[17] Quoted in *Dietrich Bonhoeffer: A Spoke in the Wheel by Renate Wind*, translated by John Bowden (Grand Rapids: William B. Eerdmans Publishing Company, 1992), 79.

[18] Kay, John. Obliquity: *Why Our Goals Are Best Achieved Indirectly* (New York: Penguin, 2010), 26.

[19] Kawasaki, Guy. *The Art of the Start: The Time-Tested, Battle-Hardened Guide for Anyone Starting Anything* (New York: Portfolio, 2004), 5.

[20] Bourque, Andre. *"Are Millennials the Most Generous Generation?"* Entrepreneur March 29, 2016. https://www.entrepreneur.com/article/271466.

MarksJarvis, Gail. "Millennials: Saving $1 million is easier than you think." *Chicago Tribune* August 5, 2016. http://www.chicagotribune.com/business/columnists/ct-marksjarvis-millennials-retirement-millionaires-0807-biz-20160805-column.html.

McDade, Sean. "Millennials and Banking: What the Data Reveals about Delivering a Great Customer Experience" *Salesforce* August 26, 2016. https://www.salesforce.com/blog/2016/08/millennials-banking-data-great-customer-experience.html.

[21] For a powerful approach to developing an effective finance plan that will empower you to live on what you make while also building a nest egg for future investment and/or entrepreneurism, see Chapter 8 of *Launching Leaders: An Empowering Journey for a New Generation by Steven A. Hitz.*

[22] "50 Tony Robbins Quotes on Personal Power, Motivation and Life." *Everyday Power* April 6, 2016. https:// everydaypowerblog. com/tony-robbins-quotes/.

[23] Brown, Brené. *Daring Greatly: How the Courage to Be Vulnerable Transforms the Way We Live, Love, Parent*, and Lead (New York: Avery, 2012), 2.

[24] Horowitz, Alana. "15 People Who Were Fired Before They Became Filthy Rich." *Business Insider* April 25, 2011. http://www.businessinsider.com/15-people-who-were-fired-before-they-became-filthy-rich-2011-4.

"What teachers said about..." *The Guardian* January 11, 2005. https://www.theguardian.com/education/2005/ jan/11/schools.uk1.

Siegel, Joel. "When Steve Jobs Got Fired By Apple." *ABC News* October 6, 2011. https://abcnews.go.com/ Technology/steve-jobs-fire-company/story?id=14683754.

Setterfield, Ray. "The Beatles? 'They have no future in show business.'" *On This Day.* https://www.onthisday.com/ articles/the-beatles-have-no-future-in-show-business.

[25] Quoted in "10 great quotes from Steve Jobs" by Brandon Griggs. CNN January 4, 2016. https://www.cnn.com/ 2012/10/04/tech/innovation/steve-jobs-quotes/index.html.

[26] Gerber, Michael E. *The E-Myth Revisited: Why Most Small Businesses Don't Work and What To Do About It* (New York: HarperCollins, 2001).

[27] Collins, Jim. *Good to Great: Why Some Companies Make the Leap... And Others Don't* (New York: HaperCollins, 2001).

[28] Toume, Kamil. "There Is Nothing Called A Competitive Advantage In Business." *Kamil Toume* July 17, 2016. https://kamiltoume.com/2016/07/17/the-competitive-advantage-in-any-business-is-one-thing-only/.

[29] Collins, Jim. *Good to Great: Why Some Companies Make the Leap... And Others Don't* (New York: HaperCollins, 2001), 5.

[30] Quoted in "*5 Quotes About Leverage to Help You Push Your Business Forward*" by Adam Toren. *Entrepreneur* September 12, 2014. https://www.entrepreneur.com/article/237180.

[31] You can read about The Formula in detail in Chapter 5 of *Launching Leaders: An Empowering Journey for a New Generation.*

[32] Keller, Helen Adams. *Helen Keller's Journal: 1936-1937* (New York:

Doubleday, 1938), 60.

[33] O'Brian, Bridget, "Flying on the Cheap: Southwest Airlines Is a Rare Air Carrier; It Still Makes Money." *The Wall Street Journal* October 26, 1992.

[34] Haq, Husna. "Neil Gaiman: one of this year's best commencement speakers." *The Christian Science Monitor* May 21, 2012. https://www.csmonitor.com/Books/chapter-and-verse/2012/0521/Neil-Gaiman-one-of-this-year-s-best-commencement-speakers.

[35] Duckworth, Angela. *Grit: The Power of Passion and Perseverance* (New York: Scribner, 2016), 8.

[36] Lansing, Alfred. *Endurance: Shackleton's Incredible Voyage* (New York: Basic Books, 2014).

[37] Ibid. xiii.

[38] Quoted in *"Living Our Values - Earth Week 2015"* by Katherine Walsh. *Student Environmental Resource Center, University of California, Berkeley.* April 19, 2015. https://serc.berkeley.edu/living-our-values-earth-week-2015.

LAUNCHING LEADERS WORLDWIDE ONLINE COURSE

Did you enjoy *Entrepreneurial Foundations*? Do you want to take what you've learned to the next level? Check out Steve Hitz's previous book *Launching Leaders: An Empowering Journey for a New Generation* AND the Launching Leaders online course!

The book and course are full of content for the rising generation and the online course includes thought-provoking videos and interactive exercises—and the entire course is mobile-friendly. Start creating your future now!

Here's some of what you'll get with the Launching Leaders online course:
- A process for planning your life
- A method for developing your core values
- An approach for adopting mentors
- Action steps for "The Formula"
- An assessment on whether you're living a "double life"
- Interactive exercises to identify positive habits
- A plan for becoming financially fit
- Ideas for giving back now rather than later

Launching Leaders Worldwide is changing lives around the world. Discover how to combine proven principles with your faith to empower your everyday life.

Visit Launching Leaders Worldwide and try the first class free!

www.LLworldwide.org

About the Author

Steven A. Hitz describes himself as a Baby Boomer with a Millennial heart. He studies, thinks like, celebrates, and advises what he calls "a great new generation." As a company founder, president, and CEO, he has employed more than 10,000 Millennials. Plus, he was a lay pastor of a congregation of 20- and 30-somethings.

Steve is a founding member of Launching Leaders Worldwide Inc., which offers the *Entrepreneurial Foundations* book as well as online courses to help individuals examine their lives, identify their most important life goals, and gain the tools they need to get there—all while living true to their personal values and beliefs.

Steve is an entrepreneur at heart and has long been involved in various businesses including insurance, banking, farming and cattle, and numerous franchise operations. His business experience, coupled with advice received from mentors and other forward thinkers (Steve is a voracious reader!), helped him shape the principles contained in this book.

In 2018, Steve was honored with a Global Business & Interfaith Peace Medal from the Religious Freedom & Business Foundation in collaboration with the United Nations Global Compact Business for Peace, Global Compact Network Korea, and the United Nations Alliance of Civilizations.

He is married to the amazing Ginger L. Hitz. They are blessed with three sons, two daughters, and ten beloved grandchildren—and counting.

Contact Steve by visiting:
www.LLworldwide.org

Made in the USA
Columbia, SC
28 August 2024

40628112R00063